Developing an Effective Worship Ministry

by Tom Kraeuter

TRAINING RESOURCES
8929 Old LeMay Ferry Rd.
Hillsboro, MO 63050
(314) 789-4522

Emerald Books
P.O. Box 635
Lynnwood, Washington 98046

Developing an Effective Worship Ministry

by Tom Kraeuter

All Scripture quotations are from either the King James Version or the Holy Bible, New International Version, copyright © 1973, 1978, 1984 by International Bible Society. Used by permission of Zondervan Bible Publishers.

Cover design by Jim Needham, Hillsboro, MO

Developing an Effective Worship Ministry
©1993 Training Resources, Inc.
>8929 Old LeMay Ferry Road
>Hillsboro, MO 63050
>(314) 789-4522

Dedication

I humbly dedicate this book to Kent Henry. Kent, in your simple trust and dedication to the Lord I learned much about the real meaning of worship. Thanks for being you and allowing the Lord to use the gifts He placed within you. Your life has impacted me in profound ways and for that I will always be grateful.

Thanks to

- *The worship team and congregation of Christian Outreach Church in Hillsboro, Missouri for being so patient with me while I have learned the lessons I am sharing in this book.*

- *Ron Ferlito for his massive contribution to chapter 4.*

- *Jennifer Brody for her fine copy editing and once again making me sound like a much better writer than I really am.*

- *Rev. David J. (what's the "J" for, anyway?) Martin for reviewing the manuscript from the pastor's perspective.*

- *Lynn Weinhold for help with proofreading.*

Special thanks to my wife, Barbara, my constant encourager... you're the best!

Contents

Introduction

When I started leading worship I had a very gifted and diligent teacher. Just by watching him I learned a tremendous amount about the workings of a local church worship ministry. I learned about the importance of relationships and encouraging one another. I saw the effects of diligent prayer. I learned how to musically interact with the other members of the team.

Unfortunately, as I travel and teach at churches I find that my story is unique. Most people do not have a mentor to train them in developing an effective worship ministry. The usual method is trial and error mixed with a few tips picked up at conferences.

Over the past several years I have had the opportunity of interacting with many well-known praise and worship leaders and teachers. I have also been able to get to know numerous local church worship leaders and pastors. Through these relationships I have found that most church leaders have the same needs in the area of worship. They are looking for answers to many of the same questions. They are endeavoring to follow the Lord, but also need some of the how-to's to help them along the way.

My goal in writing this book is to offer practical, useable information for those interested in excelling in "making His praise glorious" (Psalm 66:2). Through experience and studying Scripture, I have compiled practical solid guidelines for developing an effective worship ministry in the local church.

This book is not meant to be all-inclusive. Many details have purposely been omitted. However, the principles contained herein will offer a solid foundation and framework on which you can build a very solid and effective worship ministry.

If your church is brand new or just brand new to contemporary praise and worship, you will find these concepts helpful. Even if you are a part of an established church that has been flowing in praise and worship for years, the guidelines in this book will help strengthen any weak areas.

I would suggest that the church leadership study these principles together. In this way you can decide as a team what is best for your church. Certain areas of this book may be very applicable to your particular situation. Other sections may be less so. Together seek to find the Lord's direction that you might truly develop an effective local church worship ministry.❖

Chapter 1

A Firm Foundation — The Place to Build

Someone recently asked whether my first book, *Keys to Becoming an Effective Worship Leader*, is a practical guide of what to do in certain worship leading situations. What they were looking for was a how-to book for the novice leader of worship. I explained that although they would find some of what they were looking for in the book, overall it teaches foundations. The practical ideas can be helpful but only if they are added to the proper foundation.

Several years ago I saw a multi-story office building being constructed. Many months passed after the ground breaking before there was any noticeable construction taking place. Not that there was no activity. It just did not appear that any real construction was taking place. There were people working all the time. Cranes, trucks and other equipment droned on, but it seemed as though nothing was happening. I realized that this flurry of activity with no apparent result was the laying of the foundation. Finally, after all those months of waiting, the building itself seemed to go up amazingly quickly.

It was during this time that the necessity of a solid, well-laid foundation became very apparent to me. If they had not taken the time to establish the foundation as well as they did, all of the actual construction of the building would have been in vain. The impressive building would not have stood. However, the converse of this is also true. If the foundation is solid and secure, the construction above can be less than the best and, as long as it is anchored to the foundation, it will stand.

It is the same for us in leading worship. All of the practical ideas in the world are of absolutely no value if they are not built upon a solid foundation. We can apply all of the little "tricks" we have seen someone else do, but if they are not flowing out of a deep-seated understanding of the grace of God within our lives they are worthless.

Again, the converse is true. If we understand that all that we are, all that we can ever hope to accomplish must flow out of the grace and mercy of the Lord, then we do not need to be as concerned about the practicals. True, heart-felt worship can flow even if we do not have all of the trade secrets figured out. God is far more interested in our heart than our abilities.

We as Christians often begin to shift off of our original foundation as we "mature." This is not a conscious shift but is, nevertheless, a very real one. We easily begin to think we can live our lives in our own strength. We can even begin to think we can fulfill the calling of God by our own abilities.

God's Grace

Awhile back I had one of those beyond-hectic weeks. Unfortunately, in the midst of the turmoil I had not taken as much time for prayer, personal worship and Bible study as I would normally. When I got up on Sunday morning I immediately heard a very sarcastic voice in my mind saying, "With the week that you've had who are you to lead God's people in worship?" Fortunately, I have walked with the Lord long enough and had a firm enough foundation that I knew the right answer. I responded, "No one. Just a sinner saved by grace." I shared the incident at church and we had a powerful time of worship. It was not dependent on my being good or doing the right things. I am completely and utterly dependent upon His mercy and grace in my life for *everything*. That is my one and only foundation.

Sometimes I find that I struggle with the opposite scenario. On the weeks when I do spend plenty of time with the Lord I can have the attitude of being self-sufficient. I think, "Of course I can lead worship today. I've done all the right things this week; I've been good." At times like this, just as much as in the previous case, I need to return to my foundation of the grace of God. Only His grace, not my righteousness, allows me to minister.

I am not suggesting that time spent with the Lord in prayer and worship or the study of His Word are unimportant. On the contrary these things will help solidify the foundation. But these things do not make us more acceptable to God. They may make us more effective in accomplishing His purposes, but it is only His great love and grace that allows us to minister in the first place.

A number of years ago while I was reading Ephesians, I realized anew the power of God's love and mercy within my life. "...that you, being rooted and grounded in love, may be able to comprehend with all the saints what is the breadth and length and height and depth, and to know the love of Christ which surpasses knowledge, that you may be filled up to all the fullness of God" (Ephesians 3:17-19). What a statement! Paul is saying that when we begin to understand and walk in God's love we will be filled up with God! It is comprehending His great mercy and grace that brings us fully into relationship with Him.

No matter how good I am there is still only one foundation: the love of God in the form of the blood of Jesus shed for the forgiveness of my sins in order to make me acceptable to God. If all that I do in life and ministry is not built on this foundation then the structure will never be solid. We are all but sinners saved by the immeasurable love and sacrifice of the Lord Jesus.

In developing a worship ministry, grace *must* be the substructure. As leaders, we must teach and model it on an ongoing basis for those involved. God's grace is so easy to lose sight of that we must make an effort to keep it before everyone involved in the ministry of praise and worship. We need to continually go back to the love, mercy and grace of the Lord as the foundation on which everything else in ministry is built.

My consistent prayer before ministry is this: "Lord, in and of ourselves we have nothing to offer. But by Your grace and mercy, by Your ultimate sacrifice for our salvation, You have made us able ministers of the new covenant. Let us realize that it is only because of Your love, only in Your strength and only because of the abilities which You give that we are able to minister unto You and Your people. Thank You, Lord, for Your grace!"

Being Confident and Desperate

The second major foundation stone is very similar to the first but it goes further. This cornerstone itself is an interesting paradox: being desperate and confident at the same time. On the surface this would seem impossible. Let's take a closer look.

I have found that the Kingdom of God is full of seeming contradictions. We are to be bold (Proverbs 28:1), but we are also to be humble (James 4:10). We are told not to fear (Joshua 8:1), but we are supposed to fear the Lord (1 Peter 2:17). Deuteronomy 8:18 tells us that God gives us the ability to "produce wealth," yet 1 Timothy 6:10 warns of the potential destructive power of money. These and many other concepts seem to present a schizophrenic picture of the Christian life. But are they really contradictions? In actuality they are only contradictory to the world's ideas and systems. If we really know the Lord and His ways all of these things are perfectly normal, not opposing ideas at all. God's character encompasses both ends of the spectrum. As we grow more like Him, so does ours.

It is the same with being desperate and confident. We must be and remain desperate for the Lord's strength and guidance within our lives. We must convince ourselves that the words of Jesus in John 15 are true for *us*. "'No branch can bear fruit by itself; it must remain in the vine. Neither can you bear fruit unless you remain in Me. I am the vine, you are the branches. If a man remains in Me and I in him, he will bear much fruit; apart from Me you can do nothing.'" (John 15:4-5). Apart from Me you can do nothing. *Apart from Me you can do nothing.*

I am convinced that the Lord has given me some pretty amazing gifts. But if I took them all and added to them all the gifts of the members of my church's worship ministry they still do not make me able to bear fruit on my own. It makes no difference the talents and abilities you or I possess, we still have a desperate need for the Lord of Life within our lives and ministries. Apart from Him we can do nothing.

When the Israelites were coming into the promised land, God gave them a warning. In essence He said, "Don't think you won this because of your goodness or on your own strength. I gave it to you." We too must be on guard lest we think we have done something on our own.

A Lesson From John the Baptist

This is especially true for those of us involved in the ministry of music. Music is a very powerful medium. We can easily become intoxicated by it and the effect that it has. David Ruis, a worship leader in Kansas City, Missouri, commented on John the Baptist's statement: "The bride belongs to the bridegroom" (John 3:29). David said, "The bride is the Bridegroom's and His alone. Attracting attention to ourselves and away from Christ is as offensive as a best man flirting with his friend's bride as she comes up the aisle."

When we see people swayed by "our" ministry it is easy to think that we are really something special. When we continually receive words of affirmation about the times of worship, we can begin to feel that it is because of our own abilities. It is especially at these time that we must stop and remind ourselves that apart from Jesus we can do nothing.

"For who makes you different from anyone else? What

do you have that you did not receive? And if you did receive it, why do you boast as though you did not?" (1 Corinthians 4:7). We must always remain desperate for the Lord.

Though it may almost seem contradictory, while we remain desperate for God we need to be confident. We need to be confident that the Lord gives us what we need to accomplish that which He asks of us. "Such confidence as this is ours through Christ before God. Not that we are competent in ourselves to claim anything for ourselves, but our competence comes from God. *He has made us competent as ministers of a new covenant...*" (2 Corinthians 3:4-6).

Just as God spoke to Joshua, I believe that He wants to instill confidence into our hearts: "Be strong and courageous. Do not be terrified; do not be discouraged, for the Lord your God is with you wherever you go" (Joshua 1:9). We can have a surety within our hearts that God is with us and in us to achieve His plans for His church.

Our confidence must be from God's Word, not from our own abilities. "For it is God who works in you to will and to act according to His good purpose" (Philippians 2:13). "Being confident of this, that He who began a good work in you will carry it on to completion until the day of Christ Jesus" (Philippians 1:6). "I can do everything *through Him* who gives me strength" (Philippians 4:13). "Therefore, as it is written: 'Let him who boasts boast in the Lord'" (1 Corinthians 1:31).

If we will base our confidence completely on Him and His promises and never on our own abilities, we will be well on our way to establishing this foundation stone within our lives.

Knowing God

Once these first two foundation stones are firmly established it is necessary to continually secure them. The best way that I have found to do this is to perpetually develop my relationship with the Lord.

I am convinced that it is time to "count all things to be loss in view of the surpassing value of knowing Christ Jesus my Lord" (Philippians 3:8). If the Holy Spirit is speaking anything universally to the church in the United States it is this: know God. Nothing is more important for us in this hour.

We talk about evangelism and the power of the Holy Spirit. We talk about the power of taking praise and worship to the nations. We talk about signs and wonders. But it is all just talk unless we know God. Oh sure, we may win a few victories and see a few minor miracles here and there. However, if we will really know God there will be no stopping us!

Someone once said that if we develop a face-to-face relationship with the Lord it will save us from needing to go to a lot of witnessing classes. There is no question that knowing God is the real key to His power. "The people who *know their God* will be strong and do exploits" (Daniel 11:32). But even in this there is the tendency to be sidetracked. We want to know Him so that we can have power in our lives. I suppose that this is nobler than no desire to know God at all, yet it does not seem to be the highest motivation. Perhaps we should consider knowing the Lord regardless of what we can *get* from the relationship. To know the Lord — I mean really know Him — is what really matters.

Even as I write this I can hear the cries of despair: "But you don't understand my situation. Knowing anyone, even the Lord, takes time. And time is something I just don't have!"

Establishing Priorities

I can definitely empathize with this line of thought. From the time I became a Christian I was certain that the Lord had called me into full-time ministry. Yet for twelve years I worked secular jobs waiting for the fulfillment of that which God had spoken to my heart. I never seemed to have enough time to do the things that I said were really important. Deep inside I knew that when I was finally in ministry on a full-time basis things would be different. How wrong I was.

Even today, as I am in the midst of accomplishing the very thing God has ordained for me to do, I too often find myself putting aside the things I say are of the greatest value: prayer, Bible study, personal worship, communion with the Lord. All of the disciplines by which I can know God are often pushed aside until a more convenient time.

In this hour we must stop giving lip-service to "priorities" and instead live those priorities. If it means the house is a little messier than you would like it, it is worth it. If it means that you make less money because you work fewer hours, the trade-off is more than adequate.

I had for a long time contemplated taking a personal prayer retreat. Finally I actually went away for two days to seek the Lord. At the end of the time, as I was leaving, I went back inside the cottage where I had been staying to collect my belongings. As I entered the door I felt a tremendous heaviness of heart and I fell to the floor sobbing. I immediately felt as though I had missed something that God had for me. Then, just as suddenly, I realized that it was not that I had missed something while I was there, but that I had missed something by putting it off for so long.

Now is the time. Regardless of what it takes this is the key for us in this hour: know God. There is no longer time for life as usual. We must set our course and continue on it steadfastly.

As those involved in worship ministry this must be an even higher priority. Seeking the Lord on an individual basis as well as together as a team must become a matter of urgency for us. Spending time together in worship apart from the actual service times should be of utmost importance. Encouraging one another to know God, read His Word and fellowship with Him should be something we are all seriously committed to doing.

"Therefore, since we have so great a cloud of witnesses surrounding us, let us also lay aside every encumbrance, and the sin which so easily entangles us, and let us run with endurance the race that is set before us, fixing our eyes on Jesus, the author and perfecter of our faith" (Hebrews 12:1).❖

Chapter 2

Prayer — The Stabilizing Factor

When it comes to developing an effective worship ministry people generally are only interested in the practical outworking of it: What should we require of the musicians? Where do we find quality committed musicians? How fast should we move ahead with the congregation? Where can we find good quality songs to introduce on a regular basis? These are all important issues. But the best place to get *your* answers to these questions and to find God's overall plan for your ministry is on your knees.

There is no question in my mind that the starting point for building a truly effective worship ministry is with prayer. I have walked in and out of this truth more times than I can remember during my over fifteen years in worship ministry. There are times when it is obvious that I have fully grasped the importance of prayer, and then there are other times when it almost seems my attitude is, "Prayer? I think I've heard of that concept." I have had to learn and relearn the importance of prayer in building a worship ministry within our church.

My first lesson from the Lord came almost immediately after I became a part of our church's music ministry. I had heard drums used in worship for the first time about two years before and I loved the dimension they added to the music. When I joined our worship ministry team we had no drummer so I began to pray that the Lord would fill this void in the area of percussion. He answered quickly. We soon had not one but three qualified drummers! "The prayer of a righteous man is powerful and effective" (James 5:16b).

I cannot guarantee that the answers to all of your prayers will be this dramatic. Unfortunately mine have not always been quite so spectacular. Along with the successes there have been the other times also. Often these have come when the ministry was going very well, so well, in fact, that prayer seemed unnecessary. It was often during these times that I learned some of my strongest lessons about prayer. To be completely candid, I am certain that the Lord would most likely have wanted me to learn these lessons in a different way. I have found that God seems more desirous of using positive reinforcement than negative, but He will use negative reinforcement if we make it necessary. If we refuse to pray we will most likely reap the fruit of prayerlessness.

Prayer First

Prayer must be our first line of defense *and* offense in the ministry of praise and worship. In 1 Thessalonians Paul gives the timeless command, "pray continually" (1 Thessalonians 5:17). This is to be our mandate not only when circumstances dictate the absolute necessity of prayer, but also when they do not.

If things are going well in your worship ministry then pray that they continue to do so. Ask for an increase in God's anointing on the ministry. Pray for the spiritual and physical health and well-being of the people involved. Petition the Lord for additional players/singers to train and disciple. Ask for guidance and clear direction on all that happens within the ministry. The list could continue indefinitely, and none of these are "crisis situation" prayers. Prayer must be a strong aspect throughout the entire process of building and maintaining any ministry, especially the ministry of praise and worship.

We often overlook the obvious. When we find ourselves in times of crisis we usually try to figure out what we can do to solve the dilemma. Instead, a better idea is to pray about the situation. This is also true for the worship ministry. We expend too much energy worrying about the possibility of people leaving the music ministry or what the congregation will think about a particular new song or whether we are doing a good job. Try replacing the worry mentality with prayer. It is much more effective. "Do not be anxious about anything, but in everything, by prayer and petition, with thanksgiving, present your requests to God" (Philippians 4:6).

I use one of those new-fangled electronic pocket organizers to attempt to keep myself organized. (Please don't ask those close to me whether or not it really works!) Each day I have things that for one reason or another do not get finished. As this happens, I simply change the date at the top and these tasks are automatically bumped to the next day. Recently at the top of this movable-day-to-day schedule I typed in: "pray about everything." Each day this is the first thing I see on my schedule. It is a great reminder, and the more that I do it the more I wonder how I could possibly manage *without* praying about everything.

One day in the midst of my usual busy schedule I had not taken the necessary time to pray. I looked back over the years of my life and ministry and realized that this was a fairly common occurrence. Then I made a statement I will probably always regret, "But, Lord, look how much You have accomplished through me even without my taking the necessary time to pray." Immediately I realized what a foolish statement it was, but I also knew the response: "You will never know what I could have accomplished through you *with* prayer." We need to pray regularly.

The Holy Spirit Will Lead You

There are times when the Holy Spirit will convey to you exactly how to pray in a particular situation. Other times you must simply bare your heart. Some years ago I spoke with a man who had replaced a worship leader who was stepping down. During the time of transition this new worship leader came to the realization that he and one of the key musicians were at opposite ends of the spectrum regarding musical styles. When he finally realized this, he simply prayed, "Lord, either change me, change her, or move her on." Within two months she accepted a position out of the state.

There have been times for me that were very similar. I've said, "God I don't know exactly how to pray for this problem, but I ask you to move in this area." It is okay to pray that way as long as you are sincere about *all* of the options. You must really give the Lord permission to change *you* if necessary. There have been numerous times when I have prayed like this and the Lord clearly showed me that *I* was the one who needed to change.

My experience has been that it is usually easier to discuss prayer as a concept than to pray. Jesus *demonstrated* the priority of actually taking time for prayer. He talked about it a lot, but He apparently spent even more time doing it. Repeatedly the gospel writers tell of Jesus going off to pray by Himself or with His disciples (Matthew 14:23, 26:44; Mark 1:35, 6:46; Luke 6:12-13, 9:28; John 17:1-26). Luke 5:16 tells us, "Jesus *often* withdrew to lonely places and prayed." I find it amazing to consider that if the holy Son of God found it necessary to spend time in prayer, how much more should it be a priority for us?

Encouraging Others

Along with developing your own prayer life, it is essential to encourage those involved in the ministry of worship to develop their's also. My experience has shown that a combination of encouragement, teaching and demonstration is the best way to instill prayer into people.

It is necessary for people to *see* your commitment to prayer. There are times when we gather together for prayer and I do not feel like praying. I have found that I must overcome the feeling and simply pray. It is not only important for me, but it is vitally important for those who look to me as a leader. If they do not *see* the importance of prayer within my life, all of my talk about prayer is just rhetoric.

Along with being an example in prayer, I must also be willing to teach and encourage others to pray. You will probably find, as I have, that some people need little or no encouragement to pray. Others, however, may take more prodding. Do not ever look down on those who take more encouragement. Everyone, including you and me, has different strengths and weaknesses. Someone who is weak in a certain area needs to be encouraged to learn and to grow.

Make prayer for the worship ministry, as well as during your meetings together, a top priority. It will help strengthen the foundation.

Prayer *In* Worship

Beyond the necessity of spending time in prayer *for* the worship ministry, it should also be a priority to spend time in prayer *during* the ministry of worship in your services. Those involved in worship ministry often unconsciously separate their ministry time from their prayer time. They become so involved in "worship" that prayer becomes a peripheral issue.

In the Biblical Hebrew culture worship and prayer were not two entirely different entities. Our normal way of thinking is that we have a time in our services for worship and we have a separate time for prayer. The Hebrews never made this dichotomy. We have but to look at the book of Psalms to see this clearly depicted. Again and again, right in the middle of glorious words of exaltation and praise we find a petition for the Lord to move on behalf of His people.

A good example of this is found in Psalm 144: "I will sing a new song to Thee, O God; upon a harp of ten strings I will sing praises to Thee, Who dost give salvation to kings; Who dost rescue David His servant from the evil sword. Rescue me, and deliver me out of the hands of aliens..." (Ps. 144:9-11).

Psalm 9 begins with these words of praise: "I will give thanks to the Lord with all my heart... I will sing praise to

Thy name, O Most High." The next several verses declare the greatness of God and the victories He has won for His people. Then, in verse 13, David prays: "Be gracious to me, O Lord; behold my affliction from those who hate me..." And again in verse 19, he petitions the Lord: "Arise, O Lord, do not let man prevail; let the nations be judged before Thee."

It seems obvious that David's mindset was not, "I'll stop worshipping for a moment and pray. When I finish praying I'll go back to worship." He was simply pouring out his heart to the Lord. He was unconcerned with what was praise and what was petition. It did not matter where worship stopped and intercession started. His focus was not on his actions. His focus was on God.

This is a major lesson that we as worship leaders should learn. Including prayer and intercession in our corporate worship times is vital. We must begin to walk out the Biblical understanding that prayer and worship are inseparable. This means seeing these two powerful dynamics interwoven in our services. Taking time during the praise and worship to pray can be a powerful experience for the congregation. Pray for specific needs of those present, pray for the church (i.e., leadership, vision, outreach, etc.), pray for the government — there is so much for which we can pray.

Moving toward doing this on a regular basis may involve some character adjustment on our part. We will have to realize that our music is not the most important aspect of what is going on — God is. We will need to reach a point that we are not driven to dominate all that happens and to allow time for interaction from the congregation. Allowing people to come before the Lord in prayer and petition may mean that our prominence as worship leaders may diminish. John the baptist summed it up: "He must increase, but I must decrease" (John 3:30).

It may also mean that for a season we focus more on prayer than on worship in our personal lives. You may be able to lead people in worship for hours. However, learning to lead corporate prayer times is a bit different. If we are going to lead we must know something about what we are leading.

Imparting Vision

One of the long-term benefits of incorporating prayer into our times of worship is the vision it imparts to people. As the congregation intercedes corporately and individually for specific situations people begin to catch a glimpse of the importance and value of prayer. This, in turn, carries over into their personal lives and prayer times.

When you begin to incorporate prayer into the worship portion of your services there may be some initial resistance from the congregation. "We've never done it this way before," are always threatening words. However, we must not be swayed by negative pressure. Corporate prayer will soon be as natural as corporate worship is now.

Ask the Holy Spirit to lead and guide you in incorporating times of prayer into your worship. Be open to His guidance as you proceed through your service worship times. You may just discover a dimension of coming before the Lord you never considered before.

As you begin to shore up the foundation of your worship ministry with prayer on all fronts you will be amazed at how strong and stable the ministry can become.❖

Chapter 3

Personnel - Finding People and Keeping Them Happy

One of the most challenging issues facing any church leader today is finding committed people and then keeping them happy long-term. Nowhere is this more true than in the worship/music departments of churches. Those creative, artsy musicians who make beautiful music with their instruments can often be very temperamental and difficult to work with. Most local church music teams I have encountered remind me of the group of men David gathered around himself when he was fleeing from King Saul. The Scripture records that these men were "in distress or in debt or discontented" (1 Samuel 22:2). Dealing with such people requires much prayer and much skill. In addition, there are specific steps that can be taken to help the situation.

One of the most vital keys I have found for developing an effective worship ministry is communication. Unfortunately, as I travel I have found that it is also one of the most neglected areas. Communication is an essential element in any type of relationship, especially in one where long-term commitments are desired. If there is little or no communication people are never certain what to expect or what is expected of them. If communication is clear and consistent people will remain content for a much longer period of time.

I recommend communication in every area and at every stage of the worship ministry. I start right at the beginning. Those who are interested in becoming a part of the worship ministry at our church receive a list of guidelines. These guidelines communicate two things: the necessary qualifications for becoming a part of the team and what is expected of them once they are a part. Below I have listed each of these qualifications and guidelines. Along with each one I have given a brief explanation in italics to help bring clarification.

Music Team Qualifications

This first list is the qualifications that are necessary to be a part of our church music ministry team.

1. Committed member of this church (and/or their children) — We are open to receiving special music from those who are not committed to this body of believers but the regular, ongoing and leadership nature of this ministry requires a strong commitment to

the people and leadership of this church.

If the people are firmly committed to the church their faithfulness to the worship ministry will be much stronger. I once heard Terry Kinard (see Appendix A) make a statement which really sums this up. "Music ministry is not the right of the talented but the privilege extended to the committed."

2. Spiritual maturity — As stated earlier, this is a leadership-type ministry and, hence, is ordinarily not a place for new or immature Christians.

Like it or not, everyone involved in the worship ministry is seen by the congregation as a sort of leader. Putting new or immature Christians in this role is not a good idea.

3. Musical expertise — The musicians and vocalists need to be skilled enough to follow a service which is "led by the Spirit of God." We don't want to limit what God will do simply because we can't handle it musically.

The worship leader should be willing to take the lead in this (i.e., having the necessary musical proficiency) but this is definitely for everyone involved. Please note that the level of proficiency will vary greatly from church to church depending on the size of the congregation, resources available, etc.

4. Time commitment — Practice sessions, Sunday morning preparation and ministry are mandatory. In addition, there are seminars, special retreats, and more.

Understanding the full spectrum of time involvement beforehand can alleviate many explanations later.

5. Support of family — It is important that the individual's immediate family members are willing to accept the necessary time commitment and be a support to the individual.

Never be afraid to exclude someone from the music ministry because their family is not fully in favor of their participation. If their family is not supporting them they will probably eventually drop out anyway.

6. Ability to flow with the team — Some people are very gifted musicians and / or vocalists, but for one reason or another (vocal range, musical style, etc.) they have trouble flowing with the team. These individuals are highly encouraged to share their musical gifts in other ways (home fellowship worship, musical specials, etc.) with the body.

Just because someone is proficient with their instrument or voice does not make them automatically a top candidate for the worship ministry team. Working and blending with others must be a major consideration.

Ultimately, the director of worship ministries makes the final decision as to who is or is not a part of the music ministry team after carefully weighing input from the other members of the music team and the church leadership.

Music Team Guidelines

This list explains what is expected of people once they are a part of our church music ministry team.

1. Probationary period — There will ordinarily be a three month probationary period during which the individual will attend practice sessions but will not play / sing with the team on Sunday mornings or other special functions.

By using this idea you will find out who is really interested in helping lead worship and who simply wants to be in front of the people. This period also allows time for the individual and the rest of the team to gel musically.

2. Weekly practice sessions — All team members are required to attend the weekly practice sessions (6:30 pm

- 8:00 pm). Whenever team members are scheduled to be "on deck" on Sunday mornings they will stay from 8:00 pm - 9:30 pm for the Sunday preparation time.
Including this guideline helps add to the full understanding of the necessary time commitment.
3. Other functions — The team will be expected to lead worship for seminars and other special retreats and meetings.
Again, including this guideline helps add to the full understanding of the necessary time commitment as well as offering a broader scope of the ministry beyond Sunday mornings.
4. Commitment to being spiritually prepared to minister — Our spiritual preparation has a direct effect on our effectiveness as a music ministry team. We need to come ready not only to sing and play music but to worship the King and minister to His people.
This reinforces the essential element of our relationship with the Lord. Without it, the worship ministry team will never be effective — regardless of musical proficiency.
5. Commitment to musical expertise — We need to work at our instrumental and/or vocal ability to become the very best we can be. This means a great deal of individual practice (maybe even lessons) as well as playing with the team. Keep in mind that the team will only be as musically proficient as the individuals that make it up.
This is simply a reaffirmation of the necessity of individual musical proficiency to the effectiveness of the team.
6. Commitment to growing spiritually — This too is as important on an individual basis as it is with the team. As a leadership ministry, we need to be committed to maturing in Jesus.
Never allow people to become stagnant. Encourage and

challenge them to continue to grow in the Lord.

7. Commitment to "flowing" with the team — More than individual expertise, our musical goal needs to be the ability to "flow" with the team. We need to look at our team as not just a collection of separate musicians but as a single unit with a single purpose. Our heart attitude should not be to shine forth our own technical skill but to use that skill to enhance the team as a whole. *This emphasizes the need to view the ministry as a team effort. Without this understanding deeply ingrained in each member, the team will not reach its potential.*

Keep in mind that these guidelines are not the final word for *your* worship ministry. These are simply items I feel are necessary for our church. You may use any or all of these as well as ideas of your own, but please consider your specific church and situation. There may be other things that may be very important in your particular situation. The things that may be priorities at my church might not be as important for yours. However, these guidelines should at least offer you a starting point for writing your own guidelines.

Long-term Commitment to Communication

Communicating the worship ministry guidelines is a great way to start communication. However, there must also be a long-term commitment to ongoing communication. This means you have got to do a lot of talking. Let me give you a couple of examples.

As I talk with those involved in the ministry of praise and worship I find other frustrations due to lack of communication. One of these is a last minute notice to personnel for a scheduled special event. If you have a special service planned two months in advance but the worship team or sound man is not contacted regarding their participation until the day before, you are asking for trouble. It would be much better to let your people know as far in advance as possible. Keep in mind that this is much easier to preach than to practice. A week before I wrote this section we had a major guffaw regarding this at our church. Fortunately, those involved were very forgiving partly because we have gotten a lot better at communicating in advance. Occasionally, though, we do slip up...

One of the best ways of keeping on top of scheduling is simple communication. During our rehearsal times we sit and talk. This is not just aimless discussion. We talk about upcoming events in which we are to be involved. We discuss our Sunday morning schedule to be certain no one has a conflict with their scheduled time to be on. These things help alleviate many potential problems which can occur without this type of communication.

Unfulfilled Expectations

Another area to be aware of is what I call unfulfilled expectations. As we walk through life, we each begin to formulate expectations within our mind. Although the fulfillment of these is often based on the performance of others, these expectations may be entirely products of our own thinking. Ultimately expectations can turn to disappointments if they remain uncommunicated and unfulfilled.

Some time ago I was at a church where several members of the music ministry team had some large unfulfilled expectations. Because of comments made to them by the pastor, several of the people each felt that they would become the next worship leader at the church. When the full-time worship leader left and a new minister of music was hired from another city, they were hurt and confused. It was an extreme case of unfulfilled expectations.

This was not necessarily the fault of any one person. Apparently the pastor's attempt at encouragement had gone too far and the people expected more than he was really offering. The point is that their expectations went unfulfilled.

This can easily happen within the worship ministries of our churches. One person may have the expectation of using a certain song that is very meaningful to that person. This can be especially true if the person wrote the song. Choir members may expect that one day they will be one of the main vocalists. Any member of the team may have the expectation that the idea they shared with you in passing will become reality within the ministry. Meanwhile, you may not even remember the conversation. The list could go on and on.

Again the best way of dealing with this is through communication. I make it a point to sit down privately with every member of our worship ministry team at least once each year. During this time I ask very simple but probing questions: "What is your favorite thing about being a part of the worship team? Least favorite? If you were in charge of the music ministry what would you do differently? Do you plan to continue ministering with us for another year?" And so on. I explain that there are no right or wrong answers. I simply want their input. At least a part of my goal is to uncover any unfulfilled expectations and deal with them.

I trust that by now you are beginning to see the importance of ongoing communication. Without it there will be persistent struggles, disappointments and unrest. With it, your people will remain much happier and more content.

Encouragement

The other main key to keeping people happy for the long-haul is encouragement. Without question, one of the things sorely lacking in our society today is encouragement. The accepted norm for relating to one another is with insults. Cutting remarks have become a nearly indispensable part of our vernacular. Encouragement among close friends is a rare commodity. Between those who are not so close it is usually non-existent.

Yet despite all of this, I am constantly amazed at the power of an encouraging word. A simple, "You can do it," spoken to my seven-year-old son, David, can be transforming. A brief encouraging phone call to someone who is having trouble can make a world of difference. Sharing with the members of your worship ministry team what you appreciate about them will have a powerful long-term effect.

We all have more than enough detractors. What we need from one another within the body of Christ is encouragement.

One of the best things you can do in encouraging people is to look for their strengths. Often we have trouble doing this because people are different. If they are radically different from us, it is difficult to think that they have *any* strengths. However, if we will look past the differences we will always find strengths.

One of our main keyboardists is a former Lutheran organist. When she first started playing keyboard for us her style of playing was considerably different from the contemporary style of music we were playing. However, I realized very quickly that she was not only a true worshipper but was very skilled and creative with her music. Every time she did anything that was even a bit more contemporary than her traditional background I commended her for it and encouraged her to continue on. Partly because of my encouragement, she has used instructional videos and attended teaching workshops on keyboards. She is now as comfortable playing a contemporary style of music with no sheet music as she is playing out of the hymnal. She is even teaching others. Encouragement can make a world of difference.

The Power of Encouragement

For many years I walked in a limited understanding of the power of encouragement. However, it was not until I began to really study the subject that I realized how much the Bible has to say about encouragement. The Apostle Paul apparently understood the power of encouragement. In three different letters Paul tells the churches that he is sending someone to them to encourage them (Ephesians 6:22; Colossians 4:8; 1 Thessalonians 3:2). We *all* need people to encourage us.

"Therefore encourage one another and build each other up..." (1 Thessalonians 5:11). This is not only a good idea but a direct command from Scripture. Our words of encouragement can have a mighty effect on people.

Some people have a specific gift of encouragement (Romans 12:8). However, if you are like me you will probably need to work at encouraging others. You can learn this skill, but, like cultivating any other ability, you will need to put forth some effort. Make encouraging people a priority. Decide to do it. Once you really learn to be an encourager, it is amazing how natural it becomes. You will find yourself encouraging everyone with whom you come in contact.

When we encourage those around us we are really just being conformed more into the image of our God. He is the ultimate encourager. "May the God who gives endurance and encouragement..." (Romans 15:5). "Then the church... was strengthened; and encouraged by the Holy Spirit..." (Acts 9:31). "May our Lord Jesus Christ Himself and God our Father, who loved us and by His grace gave us eternal encouragement and good hope, encourage your hearts and strengthen you in every good deed and word" (2 Thessalonians 2:16-17).

It is even a good idea to motivate each other to be encouragers. You should not necessarily be the only encourager but all should have a part in the process. Encourage one another in your triumphs, but also to go on to future victories. Paul encouraged Timothy to "fan into flame the gift of God" (2 Timothy 1:6). We all need that kind of encouragement occasionally. Encouraging one another is a major part of building an effective worship team.

Discipline and Confrontation

The best way to build is with the positive reinforcement of encouragement and communication. However, there are times when discipline and/or confrontation become necessary. It is at these times when you will be very glad that you chose to build using the first two. If your relationships are strong and positive, you will find confrontational times much easier and far less destructive.

If I have a strong, friendly relationship with my bass player, it will be much easier for him to receive a rebuke from me about his lack of prayer. If I consistently offer encouragement to my main piano player, then she will be much more tolerant of a strong word from me regarding her continual tardiness for rehearsals. Because of the ongoing positive reinforcement, the relationship will be far less likely to be greatly strained by a moment of confrontation.

Let me explain that, like anyone else, I dislike confrontation. I will do nearly anything to avoid it. However, when it is necessary, I must do it. The results of avoiding confrontation are usually far worse than the confrontation itself.

Over the years I have confronted music team members

regarding nearly everything imaginable. I have had to address issues of pride, lack of commitment, instrumental volume, instrumental over-playing, lateness, absenteeism, disorganization, lifestyle, etc. None of these were fun, but as the leader I had no choice. They each needed to be dealt with.

Through my years in both business and ministry I have never met one person who enjoyed confrontation. Unfortunately, if you are in any type of leadership position, it is a part of the job. Like it or not, confrontation is necessary, and, if handled correctly, can be a very positive part of a strong worship ministry.

There are numerous points I could mention regarding handling confrontation. A few of the most practical are as follows:

1. Do it one on one, not publicly.

2. Specifically address the problem area, giving examples if possible.

3. Reaffirm the individual's value to you and the team.

4. Be sensitive to the individual's temperament and how they respond to correction (just as a parent would with each different child).

Through a strong commitment to communication and encouragement, as well as confrontation and discipline when necessary, you can offer long-term fulfillment to those involved in the praise and worship ministry of your church.❖

Chapter 4

Establishing and Communicating Vision

In developing an effective worship ministry in your local church, a major key is vision. When people have direction they will be far more productive. Having a written plan or vision for your worship ministry can prove very beneficial. This can range from a very simple plan to one that is long-range and very thorough. This type of communication will afford vision, value and purpose to those involved in the worship ministry.

Rather than me trying to explain what I mean I thought it would be best to show you. Below I have included portions of a well-done statement of vision and purpose which I recently received from my friend, Ron Ferlito, from Columbus, Ohio.

> Overview: This vision encompasses various activities in music and the arts for both outreach and body ministry.
>
> For regular worship services, a schedule of rotating worship leaders and ensembles will enable many people to participate while providing a broad spectrum of variety in the music our congregation uses as an expression of worship. As the church grows, activities could increase to include multiple worship teams, several worship leaders, choirs, children's music groups, soloists, and other vocal and instrumental ensembles for special music. (see section II)
>
> In addition to the regular worship services, periodic special events, evangelistic programs, and concerts, etc., this ministry will provide an opportunity for even more varied activities such as drama, mime, puppetry, dance, pageantry, and outreach-oriented music ensembles. (see section III)
>
> Included in the overall vision is the concept of being a spiritual covering and prayer support for various satellite ministries involving the arts. Ministries such as a touring contemporary Christian music group or soloist, or evangelistic drama ministry...

Are you starting to understand vision and direction? And this is from a fledgling church! Wait, there's more.

The purpose of the music and arts ministry at our church is to use music and the arts in a way that glorifies God and causes people to draw closer to the Lord. In addition, we are to be aware of the effect our activity has in the spiritual realm, causing the powers of darkness to retreat and the power and glory of God to advance.

The above stated purpose should remain as an undergirding to all that we do in order to guard against slipping backwards into a "show-biz" or "busy-work" mentality.

This purpose should be remembered in all activity of the music and arts ministry including outreach events, special concerts and programs, special music, recording projects, dance or drama productions, banner making, or any other ministries we may enter into involving the arts.

Ron goes on to outline each area in its entirety. Here is part of the section entitled "Ongoing Worship Ministry for Sunday Morning and Other Regular Meetings."

The most visible function of the music and arts ministry is to provide music for worship in the regular worship services and for other meetings of the church.
• Worship Team: The core participants are those who are members of the worship team. The worship team is the primary vocal and instrumental ensemble whose responsibility it is as a group to lead the congregation in worship at the main worship services.
• Sunday morning worship service: The Sunday morning worship service should be a time set aside for people to meet with the Lord and worship Him in an

intimate way. The role of the worship team and any other activities of the music and arts ministry in a Sunday morning worship service should be to facilitate this function. It is our job to make it as easy as possible for people to connect with God.

• It is important to include music in our repertoire that represents various styles and streams of influence such as classic hymns, charismatic standards, contemporary praise songs from various sources, as well as instrumental music.

• In addition to varying the styles of music, songs should be selected that represent the themes that have been discerned that the Holy Spirit desires for ministering to the congregation. Rather than choosing songs based only on their musical compatibility, much concern should be given to using music that will serve as a tool for the congregation to relate to what God is doing and to be able to express themselves to Him in a relevant manner.

• It is important for the congregation members to realize the importance of their involvement in the worship service and that their gifts can enhance the worship time for all who are present. Time needs to be allowed for the Holy Spirit to minister the various gifts listed in 1 Corinthians 12:8-10, as well as prayers and Scripture readings.

This section continues on, outlining the vision for other scheduled meetings as well as home fellowship groups. The entire document is eight pages long. I do not think it is necessary to include everything here but I would like to share the final conclusion.

A vibrant music and arts ministry is not developed overnight. It may take years to realize the fullness of this vision. This document exists in order to clarify and communicate the vision. Its purpose is to help us see the goal and move in that direction. As we as a church minister to the needs of the people that God gives us by providing alternatives to a carnal life through life in Christ, we will see lives changed and God build His church. It is hoped that the music and arts ministry of this church will be a vehicle through which God may bless His people by allowing many to find fulfillment, joy, and abundant life as they develop and use the gifts the Lord has given them.

With this type of clear, visionary communication from the beginning, there will almost never be questions about purpose or direction. Certainly this could be adjusted as the church matures, but at the very least, it is a valuable starting point.

Again, you are free to use ideas from this proposal, but be sure to seek the Lord for His plans for *your* church.

You may want to start with a more basic vision for your worship ministry. The application forms we use for setting up worship seminars ask the church for their vision for praise and worship in their church. One pastor summed it up very succinctly: "To have an anointed, continually expanding worship team comprised of vocalists and instrumentalists who strive for excellence, live exemplary Christian lives and can lead the congregation in worship that brings glory to God." That pretty well goes right to the heart of the matter. It also is, at the very least, a great starting point.

Setting Goals

One of the major practical steps to take toward developing an effective worship ministry in your church is to set some goals. What exactly do you want your worship ministry to accomplish? How would you like the people involved to accomplish this? Who should be involved? How long will it reasonably take to accomplish your goals? These and many other questions should be prayerfully considered before you move ahead. The answers will determine what you do, how you do it, the type of music you will use, how long the worship portion of the service will be, etc. Without a clear consideration of where you are going, you will not really go anywhere.

There has been plenty of worthwhile material written about setting goals so I will not attempt to give all of the information here. However, one very important consideration is to keep the goals tangible and reachable. No matter how noble your goals are, if they are too nebulous ("We want people to worship the Lord") then you will never know when you have achieved them. Make the goals something very practical. "We will maintain an average of 30+ minutes in worship during each service over the next six months." You may want to set goals for the number of people to be involved in the praise and worship ministry. Maybe a goal regarding more demonstrative worship (clapping, kneeling, raising hands, etc.) would be in order. The important thing is to prayerfully consider what is right for your church.

Set goals and establish the overall vision for your church's worship ministry. This will give you a course of action and a framework in which to build for the future.❖

Chapter 5

Developing a Solid Song Repertoire

No discussion about developing an effective worship ministry would be complete without some thoughts given to the potential of the music and songs we use. A great philosopher once said that if he had the power to choose the songs a society listened to, he could determine the ultimate destiny of that society. The songs we choose to use on Sunday morning will influence the daily lives of the people present.

One of the major complaints from the critics of Martin

Luther was that people were *singing* their way into his theology. Luther took catchy, popular tunes of the day and attached spiritually significant words to them. Then the people went around singing them, to the point that the songs changed their way of thinking. Our songs have the power to alter the thoughts and hearts of people.

Okay, now that we understand the potential of the songs we use, what do we do with this information? The first thing to do is to be very careful in choosing songs. We must make a firm commitment to giving thoughtful consideration to the lyrics of the songs in our repertoire. Below are a few guidelines I have found helpful, along with a few specific examples. My intent is not so much to get you to agree with my ideas or to discredit certain songs. In fact, if you finish this section and disagree with all of my specific examples, that is fine. The important thing is to get a hold of the principles involved in examining the songs *you* use.

Examining Lyrics

The first thing to consider is whether or not the lyrics line up with Scripture. This is a very important point that is sometimes overlooked. Along with the obvious things (not misquoting or altering the meaning of a direct quote), you should also look at the context of the Scripture(s) being quoted. Occasionally even words right out of the Bible are taken out of context, radically altering the original meaning. Several years ago there was a song entitled "Lift Jesus Higher" which was very popular. The song was taken almost verbatim from John 12:32. It was sung as an enthusiastic song of praise, encouraging us to lift Jesus higher because then He would draw all men unto Himself. Unfortunately very few people ever looked at the Scripture verse that followed. "He said this to show the kind of death he was going to die" (John

12:33). Jesus was talking about being lifted up on a cross, an instrument of death, and we were singing, "Lift Jesus higher." We must be very careful to check the lyrics of our songs for their adherence to their biblical context.

The next thing we should check in our song lyrics is whether we really want to say them. Sometimes we can be swayed by a great melody to use a song which may have questionable lyrics. A song that has been quite popular over the years is, "Surely the Presence of the Lord is In This Place." The melody and most of the lyrics are quite nice. However there is one line in this song which has bothered me for a long time: "I can hear the brush of angel wings." Can you really? And if not, how much untruth is acceptable in our songs before we deem them unusable? Do we really want to say things which are not true? Think about it.

Another consideration in looking at your songs is whether or not the words are good quality in meaning and grammar. Songs which are nebulous or too ethereal may be best unused. Songs with poor grammatical form may be difficult for people to sing. Unfortunately both of these types of songs seem to be in abundance because of the many people with little or no songwriting ability or gifting who attempt to write songs. More about that later.

It is also good to be certain the lyrics of the songs are within the realm of understanding and experience of the congregation. Because of the changes in language usage 300-year-old hymns (or even 75-year-old hymns) are sometimes difficult to understand. Does this mean you should not use them? Not necessarily. However, you should understand that you may need to explain certain lyrics in order for people to really grasp the meaning. The old hymn, "Praise to the Lord, the Almighty, the King of Creation," almost always needs some explanation. The last line is "Gladly for aye we adore Thee." When this song is used in congregational worship the word "aye" is almost always pronounced like "I." The word is actually pronounced "A" and means "ever" — "Gladly forever we adore Thee." But it seems obvious that if people are uncertain how to pronounce the word, they most likely do not know its meaning. So what exactly are they saying when they sing that last line? Your guess is as good as mine. A simple explanation will alleviate the whole problem.

Something else we should consider is this: do the words rhythmically fit the music? Some songs have four notes on one syllable and then follow this with four syllables on one note. Songs like this can be very difficult to learn and will usually require more time for the congregation to become familiar with the song. Depending on how strong you believe the song is (lyrically and musically) this may be something you are willing to work around. The ever-popular Christmas carol, "Angels We Have Heard on High," has sixteen notes on one syllable, yet the song as we know it has survived over 100 years of singing.

The final consideration I use for lyrics is determining whom they address. With some songs, such as "Bless the Lord, O My Soul," we are actually talking to ourselves. Other songs, "Praise the Name of Jesus" for example, are an encouragement to one another to do what the song is saying. Still others address the Lord. An example of this type of song is "I Exalt Thee." None of this should come as new or revolutionary information, but I have found that we often miss the obvious. As those involved in the worship ministry, we especially need to understand to whom we are singing. Each song is different and we simply need to realize it.

Examining the Music

In really examining our song repertoire, we should also

look at the music. Although the lyrics will have more long-term impact on people's minds, the music is the vehicle which drives home the lyrics. We should carefully examine the music for at least four things.

First, we should make certain that the music is good quality. We could spend weeks and months debating the definition of good music and still never arrive at a point that will satisfy everyone. My main caution in this area is to be sure that the music is not trite. (And I won't even try to define trite!) God is worthy of the very best we have to offer. To that end we should endeavor to make the quality of the music we use the very best available.

Second, just as we mentioned about the lyrics, the music also should be within the understanding and experience of the congregation. For a generation raised on and surrounded by contemporary music, sometimes certain styles of music can be foreign. The music of many traditional hymns, if done in the traditional style, can be difficult for people to relate to. Even certain more modern styles like country or rock, can be difficult for some people. You must determine what is acceptable for the people within your congregation and area.

Next, you should be certain that the music enhances the words. Words like "Weeping and mourning and gnashing of teeth" sung to the tune of "The Joy of the Lord is My Strength" would probably not work well. The disparity between these words and melody is pretty obvious. However, often those people in charge of choosing the songs used in church do not consider how the music *enhances* the words. A good example of a melody that enhances the lyrics is "Humble Thyself in the Sight of the Lord." The song is in a minor key but on the chorus ("and He shall lift you up, higher and higher") the chord structure gives it a major feel, thereby causing the song to build and add more depth to the lyrics.

The music in all of your songs will probably not enhance the lyrics as well as "Humble Thyself," but at the very least the music should not detract from the lyrics.

Musical Variety

Finally, it is necessary to be certain there is enough variety within the music of your song repertoire. If all of your songs sound similar people will very quickly become bored. Scripture tells us to use more than one type of song: "...psalms, hymns and spiritual songs..." (Ephesians 5:19). I will not attempt to define these. I have personally heard enough erroneous definitions of these three to last a lifetime. The point is that there is enough distinction between the three to list them separately; they are three different types of songs. We also should use a variety of types of songs.

Use songs in various keys. Consistently using the same key for all songs can become boring for the people (not to mention the musicians!). Try using several different keys. Some well-known worship leaders recommend being able to play proficiently in nine keys: the key of C as well as 1, 2, 3 and 4 sharps and 1, 2, 3 and 4 flats. This will give you a full range of keys and give you the ability to use modulations into other keys to maintain a flow in your song-service.

Use different tempos and rhythms. If all of your songs are slow and in 3/4 time, you may soon find everyone in the congregation asleep. Use fast songs, medium-tempo songs and slow songs. Use a variety of key signatures, as well as songs with different rhythmic feel (latin/calypso, traditional hymn style, etc.)

Try using variety within the same song. Have the men sing a section and then the women sing a section. Even try having the children sing a section. Use just the instruments

in a certain part of the song while the members of the congregation meditate on the words. Try singing part of a song
a cappella. Use dynamics (crescendo, decrescendo, etc.) to
add variety to your songs. All of these ideas will help bring
a freshness to your music repertoire.

Two practical side-notes are in order here. First, many
people struggle with formulating a workable format for a
master song list for their church. There are almost as many
opinions on this topic as there are worship leaders. I have
compiled many of the more useful ideas for making a master
song list and assembled them all together in Appendix B in
the back of this book.

Secondly, I find a worship music computer program
extremely helpful. This aids in organizing music as well
putting it into a useable form for a particular service.

The software I use is Maestro from On-Line Computer
(see Appendix A). Such a program can be very beneficial. The
initial set-up is a lot of work. You must enter each song
(words and chords only). The average church has a working
song list of 300 - 400 songs, so this can be a big job. However,
once they are finished you have the songs you want in the
format you want them. For example, most people do not use
the music/chords exactly as they are printed from the publisher. With this program, you simply enter the chords you
use.

When the input is finished the possibilities are almost
limitless. You can change the key of the song with the touch
of a couple of buttons. You can sort the songs by title,
composer, key or tempo. You can go through the entire list,
tag the songs you feel might be appropriate, list those
songs and then make final decisions. You may then print
each song, in any key (or several keys!) you choose, by
simply pressing a button. What did we do before computer

technology?!

New Songs

In addition to managing your current songs, you must not overlook the important aspect of continually taking specific steps to learn and integrate new songs into your repertoire. Some practical steps you can take to find new songs are to listen to worship tapes, visit other congregations, share with other ministers of music, etc. Especially for new churches or churches just moving into praise and worship Christian Copyright Licensing, Inc. (see Appendix A) and Integrity Music (see Appendix A) have teamed up to compile a "Top 100" songbook. These are the most popular songs being used in churches across the nation. Additionally CCLI publishes their own "Top 25" list to keep you abreast of which songs are currently "hot." All of these ideas can be very helpful in finding songs which will be appropriate for your church.

In looking for new songs, it is essential to be aware that the Lord has a specific plan and purpose for your congregation. A song that might be perfect for another church may be less appropriate for yours. Consistently pray that you would know God's desire for your congregation as you add new songs to your repertoire. Ask the Holy Spirit to lead you as you choose what new songs will be added to those already in use at your church.

There are some tried and proven ways to introduce new songs and also ways that have proven less than effective. One good way to introduce a new song is to use it as a special musical number prior to using it in worship. The week before its worship debut is a good time for this. Another possibility is to teach the song at the beginning of the service and then use it again later. This teaching method is especially helpful with songs that are more difficult. By using either of these ideas, the congregation is able to learn the song in a less-pressured atmosphere rather than attempting to learn it as they worship.

On the other hand, teaching a brand-new song during a time of intimate worship is usually not a good idea. If the song is extremely simple, it may work, but generally, it will break the flow of worship.

When teaching new songs, there is a delicate balance in determining how many to teach. Because each congregation is different, there are no easy answers, but there are some general guidelines. If you teach too many new songs, the congregation will become frustrated trying to learn them; too few and your worship repertoire will become "stale."

The best gauge is congregational feedback. Because not everyone will be satisfied with what you do, it is best to try to strike a balance between the "too many" comments and those that say "not enough new songs." Practically speaking, surveys show that the average church introduces about 25 new songs per year, roughly two new songs each month.

Along with finding new songs from other sources, the Lord may well prompt you or others within the music ministry of your church to write songs specifically for your congregation. As leaders within the church you have a better understanding than most of what the needs and desires of the people are. You also have a comprehension of God's plan and purposes for your people. Because of these things you are in a good place to be used by the Lord to compose songs that will help bring about what the Lord desires. Be open to His promptings for writing songs to encourage and edify your congregation.

Writing Songs

In order to consider writing songs, especially if you

have little or no experience, there is something you need to first understand. God usually speaks to us and uses us within the context of our understanding and experience. Let me explain.

One of the questions I am asked most often in the area of praise and worship is, "Why are so many songs of such poor quality?" Potentially you could listen to dozens of tapes daily and find only a few "good" songs. I am not talking about songs that are used for two months and then discarded. I mean songs of quality that will last in the next century.

We do not see songs of this caliber often enough. God's people should be consistently on the cutting edge of what is happening musically in the earth. We should not have to follow the trend-setters; we should be the ones setting the pace.

I am absolutely convinced there is one major reason we do not see more lasting songs. The teaching that allows us to rely too much on initial inspiration also causes us too often to miss God's other means of speaking to and through us.

"God gave me this song..." I have heard this introduction to songs many times. It has often been the lead-in to songs that were either musically deficient, grammatically poor, or both. The truth of the matter is that the Lord may well have inspired the initial thought, but the individual did not persevere with the concept. The song falls short of its potential because of a lack of musical and poetical abilities.

In order to fully comprehend this we need to understand one of the principles of how the Lord speaks through people. The principle is this: God will work within the personality of an individual when speaking through him.

If John Smith speaks forth a prophetic word from God it sounds like John Smith. (It may sound like John Smith speaking in King James English, but that's another story.) If God chooses to speak a prophetic word through you it will sound like you. He does not, as some believe, render you unconscious and take over your mouth and vocal chords.

On the contrary, you are in control of your faculties. "...the spirits of prophets are subject to the prophets," (1 Corinthians 14:32). You are simply yielding your members to the Holy Spirit and allowing Him to speak through you. These spoken words will sound like the person who is speaking them.

The Lord will not ordinarily speak through someone beyond that person's vocabulary or scope of understanding. Scripture itself is a perfect example. Paul's letters sound like a very educated scholar. The epistles written by Peter are very different stylistically; they sound like Peter, an uneducated fisherman. And yet both are the inspired word of God. So where does this leave us with our songs?

First, we need to understand that changing, adding to or even rewriting a song that "God gave" is not necessarily wrong. Again using the scripture as our reference, God did not always simply pour words into an individual who wrote them down as fast as he could.

Luke's gospel tells us that he did historical research for his book (Luke 1:3). Historical research for the word of God?! Luke was writing about his Messiah. He wanted it to be the very best that it could be and God inspired him through his diligence. In the same way, we must be willing to work at our songs to make them the very best we can.

If this means thoroughly researching the topic of the song then do it. If it means asking someone who is more musically proficient than you are for help then do that. Don't look at the original form of the song as something so sacred that it cannot be altered. God wants excellence and He deserves our very best.

Second, keep in mind that God takes us right where we are and does not need to override our personality. Paul's letters often sound very scholarly. This is not because God just decided to speak through Paul in a scholarly manner, but because Paul was a very learned man.

It is the same way in writing songs, whether they are an instantaneous Holy Spirit inspiration or a more laborious musical creation. You will not ordinarily be able to go beyond your language or music proficiency in composing songs. Therefore it is necessary to realize our personal limitations in writing songs and attempt to improve in those areas.

This may mean you need to take an English composition class or at least learn some grammar fundamentals. It could be that you need some training in music and music theory. It is necessary to discern your weak areas and work on improving in those areas. "Whatever your hand finds to do, do it with all your might" (Ecclesiastes 9:10a).

Third, don't rely strictly on memory in these things. Feel free to utilize grammar books, music composition books, rhyming dictionaries, etc. These are tools and can be very beneficial in adding professionalism to songs.

Suppose you are an accomplished pianist and linguistics expert. You have the ability to sit down at the piano and have a beautiful song flow from you in praise to Jesus. Obviously God is glorified by this.

Now suppose that you are you (that may be hard to imagine but try). You have the potential to write the same quality of song but perhaps you need training in a certain area or help from someone with more experience. Or maybe you need to use some of the tools that are available. Will this thought-out, worked-at song glorify God? Yes, it will!

I do not believe that the Lord prefers one of those songs

over the other. As long as they are each coming from a pure heart, God is blessed by both. In the final analysis, the Lord accepts us right where we are. But He desires for us to seek improvement to glorify Him in the best way that we can.

Copyrights

To finish out this chapter on songs, let's consider the copyright issue. The easiest rule of thumb to remember is this: no copy of a copyrighted song may be made without permission from the copyright holder. The song itself should be thought of as a piece of property belonging to the copyright holder. Permission must be obtained to duplicate the song in any form (i.e. handwritten, photocopy, recording, etc.). To duplicate the song without permission is a violation of the law.

Copyright laws protect the rights of songwriters. These laws help assure songwriters that they will receive fair compensation for their works by those using them.

From your perspective, you need to be concerned about copyrights for the sake of your church. Making copies of songs, or even just lyrics (i.e. overhead transparencies, songsheets for your musicians, etc.) without permission, could potentially cause legal problems for your church. Technically, these copies would be illegal and a lawsuit could be brought by the copyright holder. This is not a pleasant thought, but nevertheless, a very real possibility.

Researching the copyrights on the 300 or so songs in use by the average church can be a project of staggering proportions. Beyond this, paying each individual copyright holder an average of $10 per transparency can be far too costly for most churches.

Fortunately, today there is a simple solution: Christian Copyright Licensing, Inc. (address and phone number in

Appendix A). For one annual fee you can receive copyright permission to use songs from every major (and most every minor) Christian publisher. Their agreement with the publishers requires some record-keeping on the part of the local church, but the time and dollar investment are well worth it. If your church is not a member of CCLI call them today.❖

Chapter 6

Forming and Working With a Music Team

So far most of what we have looked at in developing an effective worship ministry has been the foundation and framework. Once we understand these structural concepts, we still need the practical tools to make them work. Here is where we go from head knowledge to walking it out.

For example, once you have set goals as suggested in chapter four, you will need to consider some of the practical aspects of achieving those goals within the worship ministry.

Some of these things will include types of instruments to use, how many vocalists, having rehearsals, etc. All of these need to be addressed for your situation.

Instrumentation

Many people have asked me what the most important consideration is for adding instrumentation to a worship team. The obvious answer is that it depends on the type of sound you want to create. If you want a more traditional church sound your instrumentation would probably be different than if you were trying to offer a country music sound. Since I am most familiar with the contemporary style of praise and worship I will address that area.

Small churches often do not have a wide choice of instruments available. The best place to start, then, is with a simple accompaniment instrument. Either piano/electronic keyboard or guitar work best because they are standard instruments in contemporary style music. These instruments can incorporate all three basic components of music: melody, harmony and rhythm. Other instruments can enhance one or two of these areas but not all three. Other less-satisfactory possibilities are within the same families: other keyboard instruments (organ, harpsichord, etc.) or other chorded stringed instruments (mandolin, autoharp, etc.).

Many churches use a single accompaniment instrument for their worship. A skilled, sensitive player can offer much in the way of dynamics and accompaniment style to help make up for the lack of instrumentation. At the very least, one accompaniment instrument is a starting point for building a worship music team.

The Rhythm Band

The next step is what is known as the rhythm band. This

consists of piano/electronic keyboard(s), guitar, bass and drums. These instruments offer a solid musical foundation and serve as a base for any instrumentation you may want to add later. Many churches use this rhythm band concept with no further instrumentation. With musicians who are skilled enough, these four can produce a full, contemporary sound.

After the rhythm band, your next step depends on your goals, church size (congregation and sanctuary) and resources. A small church may be very content with a skilled piano player, a drummer and a bass player. A large church may want to develop a church orchestra. Neither of these is necessarily more correct as an absolute. Correctness in this case depends on the situation and circumstances.

You might consider adding a flute or a violin or a saxophone. Single-note instruments such as these can add a great deal to your music. Enhance a quiet time of meditation during the worship with the soft melodic tones of a flute. Augment an aggressive instrumental section with a forceful sax.

Many churches have found a brass section to be very beneficial in adding dynamics to the music. Horns can work well to portray the majesty and splendor of God. They can add an excitement and intensity to the music which is difficult to otherwise achieve. Skilled players can also add a solid dimension to mellower songs. A good starting point for adding a brass section is two trumpets and a trombone. You can then supplement additional horns as they become available.

One major consideration in all of this is that many solo instruments use music written in different keys. For example, the trumpet is a C instrument. Therefore if you are playing in the key of F on the guitar or piano, the trumpeter(s) will need music in the key of G. This simple fact often limits which instruments a church is able to use. If you find instrumentalists who can transpose their own music or who can play without music, snatch them up quickly. They are definitely worth their weight in gold.

Electronic Technology

In recent years technological advancements in electronic keyboards have created other possibilities for instrumentation. The quality and variety of sounds (voices) currently available are remarkable. Other advances such as keyboards which can be "split," offer the player the option of playing a different instrument in each octave of the keyboard. For variety and flexibility, up-to-date electronic keyboards are amazing.

Programmable drum machines offer new possibilities for drummer-less churches. Even if you have a very spontaneous style of worship these machines might fill your needs. You begin by programming in several different rhythm patterns. Then, as you start the song, simply choose the rhythm pattern, tap in the tempo and, voila, you have a drummer. With a little practice, even endings and transitions to other songs can be clean and strong.

Another newer-technology being utilized by churches is sequencing. This concept is similar to recording only it is all done digitally. Many electronic keyboards today have built-in sequencers. This allows you to "record" all or part of a song using one of the keyboard's voices. You then have the option of "layering" another voice on top of the first. Most sequencers offer you at least eight different "tracks." In this way you can sequence an entire song using the keyboard voices and make it sound as though it was recorded using piano, drums, bass, trumpets, etc. Some churches are using this concept to sequence their worship songs. This can add a quality dimension to the music performance but can hinder spontaneity. Here again there is no right or wrong answer. It depends on your situation.

Vocalists

Another major area that churches struggle with is the number and type of vocalists to use. Many churches simply find people with pleasant voices and utilize them. This may work to some extent but there should be more thought given to finding the right vocalists for your situation. Good vocal quality is only one consideration. If your only singers are four very talented sopranos, there will be something lacking in the vocals. Using people with various ranges will offer some diversity to the sound. The traditional S-A-T-B works well in most cases. This may seem obvious, but some churches never give any thought to the vocal range of their singers.

Harmonies add a lot to the worship music performance. If you intend to use harmonies you will either need music with scored harmonies for the songs or people who can harmonize by ear. In either case, they will need time to work on their harmonies. This means that during the regular rehearsal or separately, there should be time allowed for working out and polishing the harmonies.

Each of the vocalists on the platform should be miked. Depending on your sound system and budget some may need to share mics, but it seems unnecessary to have them in front if they cannot be heard. Their voices need to be coming through the P.A. system.

In addition to the miked vocalists, many churches use a choir during praise and worship. A good, strong choir can add to the overall sound in worship. The choir can also act as a catalyst by being a real example in worship. An enthusiastic choir can help motivate the entire congregation to whole-heartedly worship the Lord.

Rehearsals

Some of the most common questions I am asked at worship seminars center around worship team rehearsals. How often should we meet together? For how long? What types of things should we include in our rehearsals? Should everyone meet together or should the singers and instrumentalists be separate from one another? There are no one-size-fits-all answers to these questions, but we can consider some general guidelines.

Most churches find that a once per week rehearsal works well. Some meet every other week, some twice per week. Keep in mind that even top quality musicians need to rehearse together to really sound "tight" musically. With no practice time the music will suffer.

At our church we have two rehearsals per week. Please don't tell my music team this — they don't know it. You see we have our official practice time on Saturday nights. Then we meet early on Sunday morning to run through the music we plan to use. This Sunday morning time is not really billed as a rehearsal, so it is not thought of as such. If my musicians ever found out that we really do have two rehearsals each week there is no telling what could happen! Use a little creativity. There are lots of ways to make having rehearsals more palatable. (One of my favorite punctuation symbols is the smiley face, and if I could just figure out how to get my computer to typeset it there would be one after that last sentence.)

What should happen at each rehearsal depends on the individual church. Some of the things which I recommend are as follows:

Praise and Worship — Many music leaders do their

team members a disservice by never having a time of worship during rehearsals. If we only spend time practicing *music* we are sending the wrong message to our people. In essence we are telling them that music is the important thing; worship is something for Sunday mornings. It is vital to spend time worshipping the Lord during your practice sessions.

Prayer — Go back and reread chapter 2, then begin to incorporate more prayer into your rehearsals.

Learning new songs — This one should be obvious, but please note that I intentionally placed it third in this list. Learning new songs is very important, but only when it is in proper perspective.

Rehearsing old songs — Especially as new members are added to the worship team it is necessary to go back and rehearse older songs. You may be very familiar with those older songs but that does not mean that everyone else knows them.

Evaluation of previous services — Occasionally it is beneficial to prayerfully consider the good and not-so-good things that happen during your services. Discuss them together. The perspective of others on the music team may help formulate how you handle future situations together.

Discussion (upcoming events, scheduling, etc.) — After the section on communication, this should be obvious.

Each of these items is important but each is not necessarily an absolute for every rehearsal. Plan what you will do during your practice time, but be open to changes by the Holy Spirit. At one of our rehearsals we spent nearly the entire time praying for one of the team members who was going through a *really* rough time. There is no way to schedule this kind of event, but it is vitally important to be open to something of this nature happening. The resulting family-type relationship from that single incident of prayer during our rehearsal session is still evident on our worship team.

The *length* of your practice times will also depend on your structure and goals. Worship rehearsals in the average church range from one to three hours. Although the time frame will depend on how much you plan to accomplish, the amount of time should be fairly consistent. This allows families to know what to expect.

Our rehearsals are held on Saturday evenings. From 6:30 until 8:00 we have our general rehearsal. During this time we do any or all of the things listed above. At 8:00 the people who are not scheduled to minister the next day are allowed to leave. Also at this time the pastor, and anyone else who has a significant part in the service the next morning, joins us for prayer and planning of the service. During this segment we discuss the order of the parts of the service. We talk about whether the main time of worship should be before or after the sermon. All of the various aspects of the service are considered. When we are finished praying and talking, we prepare musically by practicing the songs we are likely to use. We endeavor to end this portion of our rehearsal time by 9:30.

On Sunday morning we have another time of preparation. Our first service is at 8:00, so the music team meets together at 7:15 to put final touches on the music we are planning to use. After this we break for a time of prayer. When the service starts we are both spiritually and musically prepared to minister.

Platform Arrangements

While on the subject of music and musicians we should consider physical layout of the worship band. Many churches I visit have their musicians set up in such a way that communication between them is next to impossible. It is important for the instrumentalists to be able to communicate regarding keys, tempos, rhythms, chord progressions, etc. This communication is much simpler if the musicians are within close proximity to one another.

In many churches the piano and electronic keyboard or organ are positioned on opposite sides of the platform area. From an aesthetic point of view this arrangement is very nice. Musically, however, it is awful. Keyboardists should be able to interact with one another. Position keyboards close together.

Another common platform mistake is to place the drums off in a far corner, away from the other musicians. Often this is done because of the volume of the drums. The rationale is that the further away they are from the other instruments and the congregation, the less overwhelming the drums will be. This concept makes some sense, but again, musically this set up is terrible. Drums should be positioned near the other instruments, especially the bass player, with good visibility of the rest of the rhythm band. The sight-line between the drummer and the worship leader must also be unhindered. If you have ever encountered competing tempos during worship you will understand this point. If the drum volume is indeed a problem then there are two practical options: plexiglass sound baffles (goboes) or good quality electronic drums. Either should solve the volume dilemma adequately.

The ultimate platform set-up is to have all musicians positioned in such a way as to allow for good communication. Your rhythm band should be in a tight grouping, with others positioned to also allow the necessary interaction. This makes it possible for the worship leader or other instrumental leader to give cues to everyone.

If the worship leader is the one signalling the musicians regarding endings, repeats, etc., his position on the platform should be carefully considered. Having him positioned at middle front with all the instrumentalists scattered to either side makes communication extremely difficult. Consider having this person on the side instead. This way he can see and communicate with all of the instrumentalists without waving his head back and forth. This location may not be as aesthetically pleasing, but it is far more functional for the purpose of creating good quality music.

Along with the worship leader's position in relation to the other musicians, his proximity to the congregation is also important. In some churches the worship leader is so far away from the people that he really has little opportunity for any interaction with them. If he is really committed to leading the congregation in worship he should be as close to them as is feasibly possible.

For many churches, another major platform consideration is the positioning of the overhead projector. It must be arranged in such a manner as to allow the congregation to easily view the words, but it should not interfere with the musicians. I have been in some churches where the projector was actually shining in the eyes of some of the singers or instrumentalists. A little thought and planning can help tremendously.

In considering platform arrangements the important consideration is practicality. What will best help the musicians to do well and enhance the overall worship? Simple, thought-out positioning of your worship team members can benefit your church's corporate worship immensely.

Supplemental Ministries

At this point it may be helpful to discuss the people

involved in the worship ministry besides the instrumentalists and singers. The two main groups to consider are sound
personnel and overhead transparency/slide projector oper-
ators. Both are integral to a smooth-flowing service. Both
need to be seen as part of the overall team. Because of this
you should write guidelines for them, just as you would for
the musicians. Determine what is important for your church
and how you want them to function in their setting.

Guidelines for the overhead transparency/slide projector operator(s) should include specific instructions. Discuss
everything from when to project the songs (should the words
be projected prior to the start of the song or after the song is
started), to finding and filing the songs, to when the projec-
tionist should arrive for the service.

Sound personnel often require even more communication and training. Everything from the basics (understanding
sound and sound equipment) to more subjective areas
(proper microphone set up and mixing techniques) should
be considered. Some churches select a sound crew chief (or
coordinator) who is responsible for training, scheduling and
supervising the crew. I have found that having a person to
fill this position releases me as the primary worship leader
to concentrate on leading the rest of the worship team.

To go into detail on sound and overhead personnel would
take far more space than this book will allow. However, please
keep in mind that, just as with the music team, communication
will be a major factor in keeping people happy.

Sound Systems

When considering possibilities for your church sound
system many factors need to be weighed. The style of music
to be used, the number of instrumentalists and vocalists you
plan to utilize, and the acoustics, and the size and configura-

tion of the sanctuary are some of the major considerations. Unless you have a background in room acoustics and sound reinforcement you will probably want to enlist some help in designing and building a sound system for your church. I have listed a couple of very capable organizations in Appendix A in the back of this book.

Because of the huge number of variables for each church, as well as the tremendous amount of different types of equipment available, I will not go into sound system specifics. Attempting to do so would take an entire book by itself. However, I will offer one very important rule for purchasing sound equipment. This policy, if followed, will have great benefit for the worship ministry and the congregation. The rule is simple: always purchase the absolute best equipment you can afford. "Oh sure, that's easy for you to say. You don't know our church deacons (or treasurer or pastor or ...)." Before you consider closing this book and giving up on any more of my advice allow me just one sentence to explain my position. It is much easier to explain a high price one time than to apologize for the poor quality over and over.

Please note that I said to get the best you can afford. Obviously a church of 5,000 can probably afford a bit better sound system than a church of 50. However, never compromise the quality just to save a few dollars. You will *always* be sorry later on. From mic cords to mixer boards, invest in the best equipment you can afford.

Again, unless you really have a tremendous amount of knowledge in the area, you will do well to get some help. Find a competent sound system designer who understands acoustics. Explain your current needs as well as future plans as fully as possible. By doing this you are more likely to end up with a sound system which will serve you well for many years.❖

Chapter 7

The Worship Service

In the last chapter we considered some of the practical aspects regarding the team. Now let's look at some of the practical areas of an actual service. First, let's focus on preparing for a service.

Preparation

At seminars and conferences I am frequently asked

whether it is okay to prepare ahead of time. The question stems from the teaching that the Holy Spirit's leading must be spontaneous. However, this teaching has no basis in Scripture.

It seems that very often in life, when we learn new truths in a certain area, we tend to discard all of our former ideas and concepts and totally embrace only the new ideas. This happens in business, in life in general, and even in our churches. Many Christians, having found new freedom in the Holy Spirit, have thrown out former ways of doing things in order to be "led by the Spirit."

Today, normal Christian thinking often equates spontaneity (especially in worship) with "flowing in the Spirit," and planning ahead of time with lack of life. The concept seems to be that a worship leader who does not plan ahead will be led by the Spirit. This idea, although it sounds acceptable, is not scriptural. Nowhere does the Bible tell us that being spontaneous will guarantee being led by the Holy Spirit. Neither does it tell us that we cannot be led by God when planning ahead. In fact, we find just the opposite. God Himself had a plan from the beginning of time for the redemption of mankind. It was not a last-minute thought; He had it planned from the foundation of the earth (Revelation 13:8).

In 2 Chronicles 20, God's people were about to be attacked by three foreign nations. Under the leadership of Jehoshaphat, the people sought God about what they were to do. They did not wait for a spontaneous word in the midst of battle — they asked the Lord beforehand. There are numerous other examples in Scripture of this same thing happening. The important thing to remember is that being led by the Spirit simply means that God is guiding. It does not always have to be an immediate spontaneous revelation for the situation in which you are involved. God can give you guidance ahead of time just like He did for Jehoshaphat. It is safe to assume that God knows what He wants to accomplish on a given Sunday morning by at least Saturday night — maybe even sooner.

There is a balance to this. The main reason many people have thrown out the concept of planning is usually because they have seen and participated in lifeless "worship services" where everything was overly ordered. Probably the Lord moved mightily in a service, and, rather than seeking Him for the next service, the leadership just repeated the same format. This then became their standard method of operation for all of their services and replaced being led by the Holy Spirit.

In planning for a given service we must always remember that our number one priority is to seek God's guidance. Do not get caught in the trap of relying on what has worked in the past. Without a fresh anointing from the Lord, without a fresh understanding of His will for a given service we are really only just going through the motions.

Also remember that God will not always reveal everything ahead of time. This may be because we are not "tuned-in" enough to His voice to hear everything beforehand. Regardless, we need to be open to the leading of the Holy Spirit anytime — even during the service. This means that we cannot be so locked into our prepared list of songs that there is no room for the Lord to change the direction. Obviously, if we have truly sought His leading beforehand, this would be the exception rather than the rule, but it does happen.

Another important consideration is that a music/worship leader can only be as spontaneous as his level of musical proficiency allows. He cannot be expected to lead a song he does not know or one he cannot handle musically. The repertoire of the average church is between 300 and 400 songs. To memorize this many songs accurately, especially for a volunteer or part-time worship leader, is a monumental task.

In understanding all of this then, preparing a list of songs prior to the service is the best way to be prepared. Seek the Lord and His direction for the service, then choose the songs which will best accomplish His purposes.

Beyond the idea of the worship leader having a list it is also very helpful for a worship team. Very few churches, especially smaller ones, have the luxury of a team of musicians who can all play extremely well by ear. Because of this it is very beneficial for them to have music for the songs. If they must page through 300 songs to find the right song they might not be ready to play until the song is over. Obviously, some proficiency in playing by ear is a good idea in case there is a deviation from the song list, but to expect everyone to play every song by ear or from memory is unrealistic.

So where does all this leave us? I would suggest several ideas:

1. Seek God ahead of time for His direction.

2. Discuss your thoughts with the pastor and others involved in leadership of the service and plan the format of the service (worship at the beginning of the service followed by announcements, or worship after the sermon, etc.)

3. Pray immediately before the service and again check your song list.

4. During the service be open to revisions and changes which God may desire to make in your list.

Whatever methods you find that work for you, do them whole-heartedly. Remember: you will grow in your ability to lead praise and worship regardless of your current abilities or lack of them.

The Start of the Service

A primary consideration for starting the service is to focus the attention of the people on the Lord. Unfortunately, there is no definitive way of doing this from Scripture, but we can look at some practical considerations.

One of the best ways I have found to begin the service is with a simple prayer of repentance. Jesus said, "I am the door" (John 10:9). If we are going to come before God the only way is through the shed blood of Jesus. Sharing this simple scriptural concept in a fresh way and then allowing time for the people to repent can be very powerful at the start of the service.

Beyond this basic understanding of coming into the presence of the Lord, we also need to comprehend another simple truth. It is usually accurate to assume that not everyone is coming into the service with their hearts and minds focused on the Lord. People's thoughts are ordinarily running the full gamut of human emotions and cares. Some are joyful; some are tired; some may have encountered serious tragedy. All of these people need to be refocused toward God. For some, this will mean only a slight readjustment, but for others this could require a major shift.

How this is accomplished can vary as much as the people themselves. There is no easy answer that will work in every case. What is required is a worship leader that is listening to the voice of the Holy Spirit. This includes listening beforehand in preparation as well as during the service.

Sometimes you may feel led toward fast, lively songs which guide people by word and music into a singleness of heart and mind. Other times, you may be led to start with a Scripture reading. Still other times, you might begin with a simple chord progression and allow people to sing their favorite Scripture passage. There are no concrete rules to follow. Here are some other possibilities.

•The pastor can welcome the people after the first song(s) and share his heart about the direction of the service.

•The worship team can do one or two songs and then use a short exhortation to encourage the people.

•After a medley of songs, have the people greet one another in the love of the Lord.

•Use a responsive phrase or Bible reading. I sometimes give a different verse of Scripture to each vocalist to read at a given point, one after another in succession.

•Start with one or two "gathering-in" songs and save the main portion of worship for after the sermon.

The main point is to get the people's focus off of themselves (or their circumstances) and on to God. Ask the Lord to guide you for each particular service, and He will.

"Flowing" Style of Worship

In actually leading a worship service there are several things to be aware of. First, praise and worship music is a powerful medium. Not only does Scripture tell us that God resides in our praises (Psalm 22:3), but the music also acts to gather and focus peoples' attention. One of the main goals during worship is to hold the attention of the people on the Lord. In this way He can touch their hearts and lives in the way He wants to.

If we are going to do this, we should be aware of one of the strongest tools available. Many churches today are finding that using a "flowing" style of praise and worship will help focus the congregation on God for a longer period of time. Utilizing this style means that the music is almost non-stop. By maintaining a continuous flow you are creating a comfortable atmosphere for the people to center in on the Lord. There are very few breaks in the music to distract their attention.

Using medleys of songs helps make this type of praise and worship flow. Good medleys are usually made of two or more songs in the same key or key range, the same tempo and rhythm, and along the same theme. These songs can range from contemporary choruses to traditional hymns. The important thing is that musically and thematically they fit together to maintain a flow.

In order to maintain a flow throughout, you will need to work on smooth key changes and tempo changes. With practice and good communication (consider using a few standard hand signals to warn musicians of changes) this will become standard fare.

Open Worship Chord Progressions

Along with using medleys of songs it is good to allow people to occasionally sing spontaneously unto the Lord. This can be a simple from-the-heart song of praise or a favorite Scripture passage. In either case, using a chord progression as a foundation will enable the people to sing freely in worship. In doing this, it is essential, especially at first, to keep the chord progressions simple. Later, as the people learn to follow the basic patterns, you may then use progressions with a bit more complexity.

Open worship (or freestyle worship) is an uplifting time for the Body of Christ. This is the time when we express our hearts to the Father, not worrying about how we sound. It is a time when we can tell Him the deepest things that are in our hearts through singing a melody that is personally our own. Worship leaders and players can help draw out the melody that is in the hearts of the people by laying the foundation of a simple chord progression.

In creating chord progressions for open worship, a general rule to follow is to maintain a common note in each chord. This is called a "pedal point" and simply means to hold one note while playing over several chord changes. An example of this would be to play a "C" note in the bass and to keep that as you play first a "C" chord, then a "Bb" chord, then an "F" chord, and back to a "C" chord. The "C" note, when held as pedal point, becomes a different influence in each chord:

- It is the root of the "C" chord - C,E,G.
- It becomes the second of the "Bb" chord - Bb,C,D,F,(Bb).
- It is the fifth of the "F" chord - F,A,C.

The final effect is a pleasant, easy-to-follow sound. It is not necessary to always use a pedal point in your chord progressions, but it can be very helpful when you first start using them. This allows people who are not very skilled in singing to hold a single note and still follow what is happening.

A few simple worship chord progressions I like are as follows:

1. C - F - (C)
2. C - Dm - Em - F - (C)
3. C - Bb - F - C
4. C - Ab - Bb - C
5. C
6. repeat the last line of the song using the relative minor as the "turn around")

Note: each of these progressions are in the key of "C." They can very simply be transposed to any key you are using. Each chord symbol should receive the same number of beats (usually one measure). A final chord in parentheses indicates the final resolution chord and should not be counted in the progression itself.

Remember: simplicity makes it easier for people to follow the open worship. Be sure not to make your chord progressions so busy that they become distracting. Chord "progression" number five above is about as simple as you can get, but it can be very effective.

Be Prepared

No matter how much preparation or how skilled and proficient the worship team, there are occasional problems. Anyone who has never experienced some sort of glitch with the P.A. system has not been involved in worship ministry very long. Broken guitar strings and missing overhead transparencies (is our church's transparency box the only one with a "black hole"?) are simply a part of life. The important thing is that you should be prepared to deal with the problems when they arise.

In all of these situations, always remember that your purpose is to help focus the people on the Lord. If fixing the problems causes more of a distraction than ignoring it, then ignore it. However, you should go ahead and remedy the situation if you can do it with little or no distraction. Being prepared to deal with the problem will make it more pleasant for everyone.

I still recall the first time I broke a guitar sting while leading worship. It was quite unnerving. You can be prepared for broken guitar strings by practicing with only five strings on your guitar. Then replace the missing one and remove a different one. Of course you will need to adjust the tuning, but at least you will be ready for the strange feel of the fretboard.

Missing transparencies can be a major problem unless

you are comfortable speaking each line before it is to be sung. This takes a bit of practice and can throw off your timing if you are not prepared. However, with a little work you can do it.

Problems with the sound system can also be very distracting. Your sound person(s) should be prepared to deal with any difficult situation which may arise during the service. If the main worship leader's microphone is not working, the sound man should be ready to replace the chord and/or mic. If the monitors stop functioning, someone from the team should be prepared to go talk to the sound engineer to let him know.

There are plenty of other specific examples which I could share. The important thing to remember is that if you are ready for the unexpected you will be less likely to be hindered if it occurs. Do not focus your faith on it happening, but do be prepared in case it does.

These are a few of the major principles to be concerned with for the actual service. As I stated in the introduction, this book is not meant to be all-inclusive. I am providing these foundational and structural concepts; feel free to add your own finishing touches. If I tell you exactly how I do everything, then many local church worship ministries would end up just like the one at our church. Although I think we have done a pretty good job, making carbon copies of our ministry is not God's plan for everyone else. Use these ideas as a starting point from which you can continue to build the local church worship ministry God wants in your church.❖

Chapter 8

Training Others — A Biblical Mandate

A few years ago when I was the managing editor of *Psalmist* magazine we did a survey asking primary worship leaders to list their top five job functions. They were not to include the "spiritual" aspects (i.e., seeking the Lord for a particular service, praying for the people, etc.). We requested only the practical outworking of the job and we listed approximately 20 possibilities with spaces to list others if necessary. Much to my dismay, only 25 per cent said that *one* of their top *five* responsibilities was the ongoing training of people in the ministry of praise and worship. Only one in four saw discipling others as a high priority.

Some may balk at the idea of discipling because of the negative connotations of the word. I am not referring to the heavy-handed movement of several years ago that caused such furor within the body of Christ. I am simply talking about training people for life and ministry. The trendy word today is "mentoring." Whatever term you prefer the point is that it is essential.

From my experience it appears that discipling others in any type of leadership position is a too-often-neglected task. Jesus took his disciples with Him, showed them what to do, sent them out to do it, and then brought them back together for more training. Finally, after three years of daily discipling, they were ready for Him to physically leave them. Our attitude today is more like, "Just go do it and I'll tell you what you did wrong when you're done." This is not very conducive to attaining any degree of confidence in ministry.

Ephesians 4:11-13 tells us that the Lord places leadership in the church to "prepare God's people for works of service, so that the Body of Christ may be built up." As leaders, we can continue to do everything ourselves or we can do it God's way — training others to fulfill His plans.

In Matthew 28:19 Jesus did not say to make converts; He said, "Go therefore and make *disciples* of all nations..." He is not looking for believers only. He wants us to train those believers that they might be able to train others. "And the things which you have heard from me in the presence of many witnesses, these things entrust to faithful men, who will be able to teach others also" (2 Timothy 2:2).

How Do I Start?

Assuming that you now understand the importance of discipling others in leading worship, the question is this: how do I start?

The first thing to do is to be certain that *you* are ready. Before you find a person to train it is absolutely imperative that you be prepared to train them. In considering this there are at least a couple of questions which need to be answered. First, do you have the time to commit to training someone? When you consider preparation time, actual sharing time, follow-up after services, etc., it can easily take several extra hours each week. If you are not prepared for this big of a commitment it may be time to readjust your schedule. The second question is this: have you thought through what you will teach them? If not, it may be time for you to do some serious study on your own. Be sure you know what you believe and why you do things a certain way before you begin to teach someone else.

Let me share a few other things to consider before beginning to disciple someone. How is the overall music ministry in your church doing? If there are sizeable problems within the ministry it may be best to attempt to address those first and then begin to train someone. Is your home life okay? If you are having trouble at home, making an additional major time commitment will probably not be helpful. Is this a hectic time of year? Avoid beginning to train someone as worship leader while you are in the midst of a large Christmas production.

If you can honestly address all of the above issues you are probably ready to begin training/discipling someone as a worship leader. So what's the next step? Go back and read

Chapter 2... *pray*!!! Pray that God will give you the right person for the task. I will share with you some guidelines for looking at character qualities within the person, but more importantly, look for the Lord's direction. It would take three books this size to even begin to share concepts of how God can guide you in choosing the right person. However, if you are really ready God will give you the right person. Training people for ministry is so much a part of His heart that He is simply waiting for us to ask!

When you have found the right person the important thing is communication. Just as you have made certain that you are ready, you must also make certain that they are ready. The above guidelines are a good starting point. Also, ask them to pray for direction and confirmation that indeed this is the right thing to do. If they are willing to be trained, ask them for a *commitment* to being discipled. This should be a specific amount of time (which can later be reviewed) to which they are willing to commit. It is important for both of you to have a definite ending point. This may be extended if necessary, but it gives a definite time parameter making the task achievable instead of nebulous.

Qualities to Look For

In choosing the right person(s) to train there are certain character qualities to look for. The first one is a proper heart attitude. Obviously their heart attitude toward the Lord is the major consideration. Let's assume that this is already at an acceptable level. What else should you be concerned with regarding heart attitude? Their heart toward you, as the person who will be training them, must also be good. Additionally, their attitude toward the other worship ministry team members, toward other leadership in the church, and toward the congregation should all be at a high level.

Secondly, their lifestyle and apparent spiritual maturity should be examined. If they are eventually to be in a leadership position within the worship ministry, these areas are vital. How they conduct themselves, even in their private lives, is something very crucial to be considered.

Along with these, commitment and faithfulness are necessary commodities. Commitment and faithfulness to the Lord, to the church and to the process of being trained and discipled are all very important. A proven track record of being committed for the long haul and being faithful day by day are some things which should not be overlooked.

Finally, their musical abilities should be examined. Do they have the necessary abilities to make worship "flow"? Do they have the experience and understanding to convey to the other musicians what they are wanting to do musically? Poor musical abilities can easily detract. However, good musicianship can be a big plus for a worship leader.

Now that I have given you the qualities to look for, let me offer a note of caution. When I was twenty I began attending a seminary. I knew I was to be there but was uncertain as to exactly the ministry for which God was preparing me. During the time I was there, one of my fellow students asked me whether I was going to be a pastor. My response was immediate, "No way, I can't stand people." I am not proud of this response, but it was my honest heart-felt reply at that point in my life. Since that time the Lord has worked an amazing turn-around in my attitude toward people. Now I am often motivated by the needs of others far more than I am by my own needs. This does not mean I am a special person, it simply means I serve a very faithful God.

So what does this story have to do with the character qualities of potential discipleship candidates? Just this: the person(s) you are considering do not need to possess all of these qualifications in full measure. In other words, each of these does not need to be a perfect "10" in the life of the individual in order to allow them to be considered for training for leadership. God can work out the weak areas. They should be strong in a majority of these qualities, but a few weak areas need not exclude them from training. If you feel strongly about working with a particular person, even though he may not fully measure up to the above list, go ahead. Trust the Lord to deal with the weak areas.

Potential Problem Areas

Along with being aware of the qualities to look for, there are two major potential problem areas that also need to be considered. The first is a major age difference. (I would consider around 35 or more years difference in age to be a major difference). If you are either much younger or much older than the person you are considering training, it could be *very* difficult. It is not necessarily impossible, but it has the potential of being extremely trying. If you are much younger their respect level for you could be very low. If you are much older they may have trouble relating to you. Again, these are not impossible situations but they could cause much consternation.

The second possible problem area is dealing with someone of the complimentary gender. If you are really serious about discipling someone, you will probably share struggles and heartaches you have encountered. You will most likely discuss emotional times you have gone through that have brought you to the point you are now at. The intimacy involved in really discipling a person can be very deep. Because of this a male-female relationship can be very awkward (unless you are both single, in which case you may find some very attractive long-term benefits from the relationship...).

Assuming that at least one of the persons involved is

married (often both are), baring your heart to another person of the opposite sex, can lead to wrong relationships. This is compounded by the fact that a training/discipling relationship often takes place in a one-on-one setting. This can become very dangerous.

Over the years I have had the opportunity to disciple three young single women. Because of the potential problems I found it necessary to be very cautious in many ways. I made it a point to avoid being alone at the church with them. I endeavored to intersperse moments of levity when I was sharing very personal or emotional moments. I was very careful both for my sake and theirs.

As with the age difference, this situation is not necessarily impossible to work with, but be very cautious. Never overestimate your will-power or underestimate the force of intimate attraction.

How and What to Teach

There is no question in my mind that the single best way to train someone is by example. The Apostle Paul made a bold statement in Philippians 3:17. He said: "Join with others in following my example." We must be willing to be an example in life and in ministry. Allow those you are training to see you interacting with your friends and family. Even more importantly, be friends with them. Let them see your life of worship unto the Lord.

Also, be an example to them in leading worship. Do whatever it takes for you to be the example they need. I usually lead worship with my guitar. However, at one point I felt that I should disciple two men on our team. Although they were fine vocalists, neither of them played an instrument. It was obvious to me that the best way to train them was for me to lead worship using only a microphone, just like they eventually would. I was extremely uncomfortable with this, but it was definitely the most effective way. I needed to be an example.

Along with being an example while leading, I also try to make it a point to occasionally review *my* worship leading with the person that I am training. We sit down together and I explain why I used the Scripture(s) and exhortation(s) I did, why I skipped a song or two on the planned list, etc. I also like to sometimes share my preparation time with them. Finding out how I arrived at the original song list in the first place can be very enlightening for someone learning about leading worship. I have also found it very helpful to occasionally sit with the disciple during the sermon, especially if there is ministry anticipated afterward. I will quietly share my thoughts on songs, altar call, flow, etc. during the sermon. This helps them to start thinking along these lines for themselves.

In sharing with a person you are training it is important to remember to share *everything*. It is so easy, especially after leading worship for a few years, to take many things for granted. However, the things that seem second-nature to you are exactly the things that a novice leader of worship needs to know. Along with these things encourage them to ask questions. If there is *anything* they do not understand they should ask. Even if you do not always have all the answers, they should be encouraged to ask. This will help sharpen your skills and thinking as well as helping to strengthen your relationship with one another — they get to find out that it is possible to be anointed and not have all the answers. That, in and of itself, is worth its weight in gold.

All of these practical aspects are essential, but do not neglect the basics. Leaders too often assume knowledge on the part of others. It may be worthwhile for you to do a simple Bible study on what worship is and what it is not. Maybe they need to be taught the importance of worship in the life of the believer. These basics should not be overlooked.

Safeguards

Before I allow a person I am training to lead worship on a Sunday morning there are some very specific steps I take. For their sake, I am very careful to build in some safeguards that will help them to do the best job possible.

The first of these is what I refer to as a "controlled setting." Our worship team is set up in a way that not everyone is scheduled to minister every Sunday. I make out a schedule a couple of months in advance so everyone knows exactly when they need to be available. In doing this I allow the first-time worship leader to choose who he/she would like to have with him/her that day. This can be very comforting to that person. For example, at one point we had a man on our team who was a phenomenal keyboardist. He ordinarily played our synthesizer, and his creativity was such that it made an obvious difference in our overall sound when he played. However, his musical creativity and understanding far surpassed most of the rest of the members of the team. Because of this, dealing with him on a musical basis could be very intimidating for some people. Bottom line: a not-overly-confident eighteen-year-old-beginning-worship-leader might not want the phenomenal keyboardist on that first Sunday. So I allow the worship leader to decide what people will be there in order to provide a controlled setting. Only the people that he/she is comfortable with will be "on" that first Sunday.

The second thing I do for the novice worship leader is to provide a "safety net": me. On the given Sunday, I am scheduled to minister with the team but I will be playing guitar only; I will not have a vocal microphone. I do have a microphone but it is pointed at the sound hole of my guitar. This is completely unnecessary because my acoustic guitar has a pick-up built in.

The reason for the microphone is "just in case." The first-time worship leader knows that at any point during the service he/she can, with one look, turn the service over to me. All I need to do is raise my microphone stand and I will be leading. The sound crew is aware that if my mic comes up I am now the one in charge of the worship. It's that simple. I have never had to take over, and I will probably never need to because I spend a great deal of time preparing people before they ever reach the moment of actual leading. But the safety net concept is worth the effort when you realize how much stress it removes from the beginning leader. He knows that if someone gives an off-the-wall "word" or anything out of the ordinary happens he has a simple way out: there is an experienced worship leader ready to take over at a moment's notice. Incorporating safeguards like these can remove a great deal of anxiety from a worship leader who is just starting out.

Along with these safeguards there are two very important keys to keep in mind in this entire process. The first is encouragement. Never underestimate the effectiveness of encouragement. Let the person know the positive qualities you saw in them at the beginning. Continually let them know the progress you see, no matter how small, as you go along. Encourage them. In doing so you are automatically employing the second key: communication. Let them know how you feel they are doing, what they might consider doing differently, what you see as their strong areas and their weak areas. Encouragement and communication are essential in training someone for ministry.

When Are you Finished?

Knowing when you are finished can be difficult unless

you have a pre-determined goal. For me the goal was simple. My travel schedule demands that I be away from my home church on a fairly regular basis. Because of this it is imperative for me to have others who can do a quality job of leading worship when I am gone. That was (and is) my goal. Perhaps your goal will be to replace yourself. Or maybe it is to send well-trained worship leaders out to other churches. Any of these and more are possibilities. The important thing here is to prayerfully consider the final goal prior to starting and then aim at that goal all through the discipling process.

For me an even deeper question than, "When am I finished training a particular individual?" was, "When I am finished discipling?" At one point I had thoroughly trained four individuals in leading worship. They all did a tremendous job of leading and I had no reservations about leaving any one of them in charge of a particular service. I was very comfortable with them and the job I had done. Then, within a two-month period of time something very strange happened. One moved to another part of the country because of a job situation. One left the team to take care of her new-born baby. One was helping another church through a major crisis and was unavailable on Sunday mornings. And the last one asked for a temporary leave of absence because he was in charge of our annual three-week Family Bible Camp which was about to begin. Just that quickly I went from four very competent back-up worship leaders to zero.

During this time the Lord clearly showed me the lesson I needed to learn. Discipling is not a one-time process to reach a certain point and then stop. As long as I have gifts and abilities given by God I must share them. It must be an ongoing process in my life. If you have gifts and abilities that the Lord has given, you have a responsibility to share those with others. Training/discipling/mentoring others must become a part of our character, a portion of who we are. "And the things which you have heard from me in the presence of many witnesses, these things entrust to faithful men, who will be able to teach others also" (2 Timothy 2:2).❖

Chapter 9

Pastors Only - The Pastor's Role in the Worship Ministry

In the book of Revelation it is the elders who are seen at the forefront in worship. Too often the role of the pastor is overlooked in developing a truly effective worship ministry. However, his leadership and authority within the church make him *the* key player in establishing the priority of worship. The long-term worship life of the church will not long-term go beyond the worship life of the pastor. The effect of his words about worship and his participation in worship cannot be overemphasized. By his encouragement and example the pastor will set the pace for praise and worship in the church.

I have had the opportunity to visit churches where it was obvious that the pastor had not yet grasped the importance of his leadership in worship. In those churches, even though they may have tremendous, high-caliber musicians, the worship time was lifeless. The people had not understood the significance of worship because the pastor had not.

On the other hand, I have been at churches where the quality of the music program left much to be desired. In one church, the worship "team" consisted of one not-very-talented piano player playing an out-of-tune piano. However, the time of worship was glorious because the pastor had taught and modeled the relevance of worship in the life of believers. The quality of the music had far less effect on the people's response in praise and worship than did the pastor's influence.

Being a Radical Worshipper

I recently heard a teacher at a worship conference make a statement that I had never really considered: "The pastor should be the most radical worshipper in the church." As I thought about this statement I realized that it really encompasses all of the ideas I have shared above. If it is true that the worship of the church really will not go beyond the worship of the pastor, then he has an automatic mandate to press the limits in his own life of worship. He should be the one people can look to and say, "There's a real worshipper of God!"

Some time ago I heard Judson Cornwall speaking at a

conference. He shared that many pastors spend the entire time of worship doing everything except worshipping the Lord. They look over the order of service to be certain of what is happening next. They recheck their sermon notes one last time. They signal the ushers or someone else to do whatever they think might need doing. Everything seems to take precedence over that which is really important: worshipping the Lord. If we expect worship to have prominence in the lives of those in our churches, then we must show what wholehearted, unashamed worship of God is like.

After seeking the Lord, the pastor of a large church came to the realization that the worship in his church was lacking. The church was very strong in teaching the Word, but praise and worship was a weak area for them. Because of this, the pastor made a strong commitment to strengthen their worship. He brought in a very gifted and anointed worship leader to help, but he took another step that I believe was even more important. He told his deacons and elders that for the next six months they were to diligently follow the lead of the new worship leader. If he lifted his hands to the Lord, they were to lift their hands to the Lord. If he knelt down in worship, they were to kneel. If he danced, they were to dance. They were to help model worship, and the pastor would do the same. Within six months the worship life of that church was revolutionized because the leadership made it a priority to exemplify worship.

In walking this out in your own church it is important to view the pastor and the worship team together as one team. They must work together in establishing the priority of worship within the church. However, simply because of his role, the pastor will always be the key player. If the pastor will take the lead in being an example in worship, the congregation will go much further in experiencing a fulfilling life of worship together.

Encouraging and Teaching the Congregation

Along with being an example, the pastor must also take the role of teacher. Just as in training children, teaching by example *and* careful instruction are both essential. The pastor should regularly share scriptural and experiential concepts with the congregation to encourage them to whole-heartedly worship the Lord. An occasional sermon or series of sermons on worship might be appropriate. Some pastors plan a series of sermons on worship once every year simply to encourage the people away from the usual human tendency to get lazy in worship.

Instructing the congregation in worship should include the entire scriptural counsel of worship. Too often we assume that since someone is born-again they understand worship. However, more often than not people's ideas of worship are formed more by experience than by the Bible. Their childhood memories of going to church fashion their present understanding of worship more than the Word of God. The people in our churches need to be taught everything from what worship is to why we worship to how we should worship. Pastors must endeavor to offer the full counsel of the Scriptures in motivating people to worship and praise the Lord. Some churches take a few minutes every Sunday to encourage and instruct the people in Scriptural worship.

In teaching about worship, the word "encouragement" should be a guiding concept. Beating people with the necessity of worship is usually far less effective than encouraging them to worship because of His love and greatness. The Bible teaches that it is God's grace which leads us even to repentance (Romans 2:4). There is something about understanding the Lord's mercy and love toward us which draws us to Him.

Carefully chosen, encouraging words about God's marvelous grace toward us will go further in motivating His people to worship than all of the law-oriented injunctions we can think of.

Communicating Direction

The pastor generally has an all-encompassing vision for his church. Every area of the ministry must somehow fit into that vision or it is simply extra baggage. This is especially true for the ministry of praise and worship. The vision for the music department must fit in with the overall vision for the church. For example, let's say the vision for a particular church is outreach to young people (ages 16-25) in the inner city. The songs used, the entire style of music and worship would most likely be radically different than if the main vision were a bus ministry outreach to those in nursing homes. Obviously these are pretty radical extremes but the point is still the same: the direction of the music and worship ministry in a local church must enhance the direction and vision of the church as a whole.

In our church the senior pastor (age 53) has very clearly communicated to me that he does not want traditional church music. He wants more contemporary style praise and worship, simply because it is the style of music that this generation understands.

The best way for the worship to enhance the overall vision is for the pastor to consistently share that vision with the congregation, the music department, the church staff and especially the worship leader/minister of music. Continually instilling the direction of the church into the key people involved will help assure that the direction is ultimately achieved. By regularly sharing it with those involved in the worship ministry, a major portion of the overall ministry will be "on board." When you consider the influence that the worship ministry has in the church (percentage of time spent in public meetings in praise and worship is usually 30-60%), then imparting a clear understanding of the vision of the church to those involved in worship ministry is essential.

You should understand that communication of this type must involve some interaction. You will be unable to instill your heart and vision into someone with whom you never have any interaction. Therefore it is necessary to meet together, at least occasionally. To me this seems like a very obvious point. However, I am continually amazed at the number of pastors I meet who never take the time to meet with their worship leader/minister of music.

Meet together on a consistent basis. Discuss the direction of the church and the worship ministry. Talk about past and future services. Consider together what went wrong with a particular service. Discuss possibilities for next week's service. All of these things are necessary in developing the type of relationship that is essential in fulfilling the vision of your particular church.

Encouraging the Music/Worship Ministry

Finally, one of the most important things a pastor can do in developing an effective worship ministry is to encourage those involved. As human beings there are few things which mean as much to us as positive words and actions from someone in authority. A note of appreciation from the boss for a job well done is always welcome. Words of encouragement from a coach or a teacher spur us on to greater achievements. This principle is the same in the church. Encouragement, in and of itself, is a great reward.

The pastor of our church often mentions the music ministry team or the sound technicians from the pulpit.

Always these times are an affirmation of the quality of ministry and the importance of that ministry to our church. The entire congregation applauding in agreement offers obvious support in a sometimes thankless job. Encouragement is always appreciated.

Even simple means of encouragement can pay big dividends. An occasional telephone call to say, "Thanks for your hard work," can be uplifting. A visit just to offer words of encouragement will be remembered for a long time.

Along with words of encouragement consider tangible encouragements as well. I still remember when I first started receiving a small salary from our church for leading worship. Although I probably would not have admitted it then, it made a difference in my attitude in that position. I was receiving at least a token of esteem for the work put forth. Please understand that financial remuneration is not my motivation in leading worship, but it does speak clearly of the importance of the position. It can be a great encouragement.

Besides financial compensation, consider other tangible means of encouragement. Give a subscription to a praise and worship magazine. Send those involved in worship ministry to a worship conference. Host an annual banquet to honor volunteers at your church and include the musicians and singers. Purchase music books and cassettes for them to learn new songs from. Offer to pay for new guitar strings. Have the piano tuned regularly. Any or all of these things are a wonderful means of showing support and encouragement to those who labor diligently week after week.

The pastor is definitely the key person in worship in a local church. His example, his communication, his encouragement will help set the tone for the congregation to follow.❖

Epilogue

As I considered how to end this book I realized the importance of reemphasizing a strong relationship with the Lord. A local church worship ministry can only be effective if the people involved are following hard after God (Psalm 63:8). Without this, all of the practical information in this book is worthless. However, if the members of your ministry team are indeed wholeheartedly pursuing the Lord, you will be able to utilize everything you have learned to its fullest potential.

Below is a story/description of the heart that is necessary for those involved in the ministry of praise and worship.

I stood before the door wanting to open it but not touching it. I knew that the door was not mine to open, yet I wanted to see what was on the other side. Then silently, as if by some supernatural power, the door opened. What I beheld was overwhelming. It was as though liquid light filled the room. The light had no source: it came from nowhere and everywhere. As I gazed upon it, the light seemed to grow in intensity and volume.

Then suddenly, without warning, some of the light flowed out of the room and touched me. I felt faint from it, as though it had some sort of power of its own, but I stood firm and it did not force me to succumb. As quietly and gently as it had come the light slipped back into the room, leaving me standing there still awed and deeply moved by its touch.

I looked again and saw the figure of a man clothed in white standing in the middle of the room. His eyes caught my gaze and I could not look away. They were lonely eyes. Not with the loneliness of knowing no people, but with the loneliness of having no one who will listen—no close confidant. He beckoned for me to come and there was something about Him that seemed to say that He had the power to make me come. But again I stood firm, and He did not force me.

It was not that I did not want to go. I did. I desperately did. But I was afraid. Afraid of what He might make me do; afraid of what I might miss while I was in the room; afraid of Him seeing what I was really like if I got too close. And as these thoughts raced through my mind, the loneliness in His eyes seemed to intensify. I wanted to run to Him and I wanted to run away, but I didn't do either. I just stood there as if frozen in place.

Then He spoke, "I want you to come and be in My presence. You will lead others into My presence, but more importantly, I want you to come and be in My presence. I want *you* to come."

The words were barely spoken when I knew what I must do. I burst through the door, but the power of the light overcame me. It lifted me up and softly placed me at His feet. I knelt there at the feet of this omnipotent One and together we wept. I knew His tears were for me and for others like me. We continued to weep; and cry aloud.

Then suddenly there came peace, and, as if on command, we both opened our tear-drenched eyes, lifted our heads and rejoiced. As we sang and danced there together, I sensed the presence of others in the room. I turned to look and great multitudes were streaming through the door and they, too, were rejoicing. As I turned back to the One who stood before me, I couldn't help noticing that the loneliness in His eyes had been replaced by joy and happiness.

We celebrated and danced together for what seemed like moments but was more probably hours or even days. And when it was over and all of the people had gone, He put His hand on my shoulder and reminded me of the fears that had kept me out of the room for so long. They all seemed so silly now. I had done everything He wanted me to and there was nothing for which I should be ashamed or afraid; I had been with Him for days and yet I had missed nothing that was truly important; I had been almost one with Him—He knew me intimately and still the compassion shone forth from Him.

Then He spoke again, "You have come before Me and

others have followed your lead. Now they have gone, but do not fear —they will return, sometimes together, sometimes alone. But you, you have remained and that is as it should be. I have called you to lead them to Me, but the calling is more than that. It requires that *you* be in My presence — often — and regularly. You must weep when I weep, rejoice when I rejoice, mourn when I mourn, and sing when I sing. You must know Me so well that you can hear My voice even when I whisper to you in the midst of a rejoicing throng. Abide with Me."❖

Appendix A

Praise and Worship Resource Organizations

This is a listing of various organizations that offer further help in developing your local church worship ministry. This is not meant to be an all-inclusive list. These are simply a few organizations with which I am personally acquainted. Each listing gives the name and address as well as a very brief description of the products or services. For more complete information, please feel free to contact the specific organization(s).

Acoustic Dimensions
15505 Wright Brothers Drive Suite 5
Dallas, TX 75244
(214) 239-1505
> Church acoustics and sound system consulting.

Beatty, Chris and Carole
The Upright Foundation
P.O Box 699
Lindale, TX 75771
(903) 882-9602
> Vocal training.

Bible Temple
9200 NE Fremont
Portland, OR 97220
(503) 255-2224
> Annual worship conference.

Boschman, LaMar, Ministries
P.O. Box 130
Bedford, TX 76095
(817) 540-1826
> Worship seminars and conferences, tapes and videos, books.

Bowersox, Steve, School of Music
P.O. Box 9309
Mobile, AL 36691
(205) 639-0639
> Worship musicians theory course.

Christ for the Nations Institute
P.O. Box 769000
Dallas, TX 75376-9000
(214) 376-1711
> A well-established Bible college with an excellent program in music and worship.

Christian Copyright Licensing Incorporated
6130 NE 78th Ct. Suite C11
Portland, OR 97218
(800) 234-2446
> Complete song copyright permission for local churches.

Dalton, Don and Valerie
1634 Prehistoric Hill
Imperial, MO 63052
(314) 464-3347
> Worship seminars.

Face to Face Ministries
917 Haidin Circle
Anaheim, CA 92807
(714) 535-5055
> Worship seminars.

Goodall Guitar
P.O. Box 3542
Kailua Kona, HI 96745-3542
(808) 329-8237
> Hand-made guitars for worship guitarists.

Henry, Kent, Ministries
9820 E. Watson Rd.

St. Louis, MO 63126
> Worship seminars and conferences, tapes and videos, *Psalmist* magazine.

Ingram Ministries
P.O. Box 10261
Daytona Beach, FL 32120
(904) 322-0020
> Worship seminars.

Integrity Music
P.O. Box 851622
Mobile, AL 36685
(205) 633-9000
> Praise and worship recordings and music.

International Worship Symposium
P.O. Box 260049
Plano, TX 75026
(800) 642-SONG
> Regional, national and international worship conferences.

Joyful Word Ministries
Charlie and Jill LeBlanc
P.O. Box 22441
St. Louis, MO 63126
(314) 225-8600
> Worship seminars.

Jubal Music
3500 Sutherland Ave. M203
Knoxville, TN 37919
(615) 558-9284

Music transcription and arranging, worship music theory correspondence course.

Kinard, Mike and Terry
P.O. Box 496646
Garland, TX 75049
(214) 771-0205
> Worship seminars.

Kingdom of Priests Ministries
P.O. Box 850311
Mobile, AL 36685
(205) 661-9777
> Worship seminars.

Maranatha! Music
30230 Rancho Viejo Road
San Juan Capistrano, CA 92675
(800) 245-SONG
> Praise and worship recordings, House of Worship new songs for praise and worship, and worship seminars.

Music Revelation
7 Elmwood Ct
Rockville, MD 20850
> Newsletter, books and teaching tapes for music ministers.

NavPress
P.O. Box 35006
Colorado Springs, CO 80935
(800) 366-7788
> INFOsearch computer programs for Hosanna! Music and Worship and Celebration Hymnal.

On-Line Computer Programming
1211 Bell Road — Apt. 268
Antioch, TN 37013
(615) 731-3135
> Maestro computer program for worship leaders.

Owens, Jimmy and Carol
School of Music Ministry International — SMMI
18440 FM Rd. 1253
Lindale, TX 75771
> Intensive training schools for worship leaders and musicians.

People of Destiny Music
7881 Beechcraft, Suite B
Gaithersburg, MD 20879
(301) 926-2200
> New songs for praise and worship.

Piano By Ear
P.O. Box 47099
Atlanta, GA 30362
(404) 391-0606
> Keyboard training for worship personnel via workbooks, tapes and seminars.

Rothwell, Randy
1123 Fribourg
Mobile, AL 36608
(205) 344-1612
> Worship concerts and practical workshops for worship bands.

Sacred Music News and Review

P.O. Box 1179
Grapevine, TX 76099-1179
(817) 488-0141
> Traditional music newsletter for liturgical churches.

Selah Songs

2511 Losantiville
Cincinnati, OH 45237
(513) 841-1722
> New songs for praise and worship, with orchestrations available.

Shady Grove Church

1829 W. Shady Grove Rd.
Grand Prairie, TX 75050
(214) 790-0800
> Semi-annual worship conference.

Sorge, Bob

236 Gorham St.
Canandaigua, NY 14424
(716) 394-7450
> Worship seminars, instructional videos and books.

Star Song Communications

2325 Crestmoor
Nashville, TN 37215
(615) 269-0196
> Heart of Worship, new songs for praise and worship and *The Complete Library of Christian Worship,* encyclopedia giving complete historical and biblical perspective on all aspects of Christian worship.

Taipale Media
1471 Colgate Dr.
St. Charles, MO 63303
(314) 946-3891
> Church sound reinforcement seminars and consulting.

TCMR — The Church Music Report
P.O. Box 1179
Grapevine, TX 76099-1179
(817) 488-0141
> Newsletter for music ministers.

Tempo Music Publishing
3773 W. 95th St.
Leawood, KS 66206
(913) 381-5088
> New songs for praise and worship.

Training Resources
8929 Old LeMay Ferry Rd.
Hillsboro, MO 63050
(314) 789-4522
> Worship seminars, teaching tapes and books.

Vineyard Music
5300 E. LaPalma
Anaheim, CA 92807
(714) 777-8027
> Praise and worship recordings and music.

Worship Congress
P.O. Box 641
Mt. Juliet, TN 37122

(615) 754-7035
> Regional and national worship conferences.

Worship International
P.O. Box 9309
Mobile, AL 36691
(205) 639-0639
> Worship conferences.

Worship Leader Magazine
107 Kenner Ave.
Nashville, TN 37205
(615) 386-3011
> *Worship Leader* magazine.

Worship Today Magazine
756 Munich St. NW
Palm Bay, FL 32907
(800) 877-5334
> *Worship Today* magazine.

ZionSong Music/Ecclesia Communications
P.O. Box 70
Valdosta, GA 31603
(912) 247-5654
> New songs for praise and worship.

Appendix B

Forming a Master Song List

An important point in any effective worship ministry is a listing of all of the songs available for use. It seems that everyone has his own idea of how this list should be compiled. There are nearly as many variations to a "master song list" as there are worship leaders.

There are no definite right or wrong answers in putting together such a list. You must decide what is necessary for you and your situation. Below are some of the more popular components of a master song list. These can be used singly or in conjunction with one another.

Songs listed alphabetically using title, first line of song (if different) and first line of chorus (if different). In listing the songs in this manner, a song could theoretically have as many as three listings. This is important because sometimes you may want to start a song at the chorus instead of the first verse.

Songs listed by key or key range. This is especially helpful for putting together medleys of songs. Using a key range instead of simply a single key can be very beneficial for modulations, medleys, etc.

Songs listed by tempo and time signature. Tempo is usually a generalized breakdown (i.e. fast, medium, slow, with some songs working well at more than one of these tempo designations). Again, this is important for medleys. Time signature is also necessary in making transitions easier. It is normally only listed on an index if the song is not in common time. Tempo and time signature are usually the most helpful when used in conjunction with the key listing.

Songs listed by theme. A listing of this type can be very useful in organizing a thematic service. For example, if you want to dwell on God's grace, a listing of songs having that theme would be extremely beneficial.

Scripture reference. This can be helpful in much the same way as the theme listing. It may also be beneficial to read the scriptural basis for a particular song before singing the song. It is usually not necessary to have a separate list by Scripture reference but having the reference with the song in another list is worthwhile.

Corresponding reference number for transparencies and/or slides. Many churches now using transparencies or slides use reference numbers for each song. This can make the songs easier to find. In using this system, it is often helpful for the worship leader to have the reference number for each song.

KEYS TO BECOMING
AN EFFECTIVE WORSHIP LEADER
by Tom Kraeuter

Learning any craft by trial and error can be frustrating. This is especially true when learning how to be effective as a worship leader. Practicing untried methods and ideas on your congregation or music team often proves discouraging. Trying unsuccessful ventures long-term can be devastating.

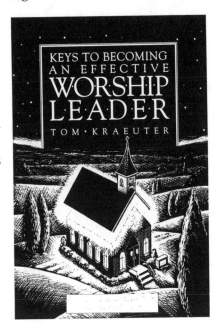

Here's help!

Keys to Becoming and Effective Worship Leader is full of valuable insights gleaned from years of experience. These practical, proven ideas will benefit anyone involved in the ministry of praise and worship.

If you long to become more effective in leading God's people in worship, this book is for you.

Here's what others are saying about *Keys to Becoming an Effective Worship Leader*:

"In very practical, down-to-earth terms Tom leads you through a journey into the heart of the effective worship leader... a journey needed by us all! While he writes from a praise and worship backgound I could find little that could not be used by any church music leader of any denomination."

Bill Rayborn, *The Church Music Report*, Grapevine, TX

"I love it! You have done an outstanding job of putting into practical words some of the most essential issues challenging worship leaders today. Thank you."

C. Harry Causey, *Music Revelation*, Rockville, MD

"Seldom have I found material that is so thorough yet so simple in its presentation. Having personally led worship for over 20 years, I found new insights and encouragement."

David Butterbaugh, Word of Faith, Dallas, TX

"Tom gives gutsy and straight forward advice that is sure to benefit and challenge even the most seasoned worship leaders. I only wish I had written it myself."

Doug Fowler, New Life Christian Fellowship, Jacksonville, FL

"...the best handbook available for those desiring to enter worship ministry, as well as a tremendous refresher for those of us currently involved."

John Chisum, Integrity Music, Mobile, AL

"... a tremendous resource for both the beginning and experienced worship leader. Tom has done a great job in dealing with the priorities of first preparing the heart and then the ministry team. A 'must read' for all those involved in the leading of worship."

Byron Lee, First Church of the Nazarene, Medford, OR

ORDER TODAY

BOOK — *112 pages* $ 7.95
AUDIO CASSETTE — *2 tapes featuring*
  the complete text read by the author $10.00

No Time to Read?

Developing an Effective Worship Ministry
and
Keys to Becoming an Effective Worship Leader
are now both available on audio tape.

Each book is packaged in an attractive tape binder.
Two cassettes contain the entire text of the book,
read by the author.

Retail price — ~~$12.00~~
Special Offer — $10.00
(each book)

Training Resources Order Form

TITLE / DESCRIPTION	PRODUCT #	QTY	PRICE	TOTAL
			Subtotal	
			Shipping/Handling	

US/Canada, add 10% on $0-$50. Over $50, add $5.00 only. For foreign orders (outside US/Can) add 40% to all orders for air shipment, 15% for surface shipment.

| | | | **TOTAL** | |

PAYMENT OPTIONS
(check one)

❏ Enclosed is my check or money order for $_____ in US currency.
(Make checks payable to Training Resources.)

❏ Credit Card
Please bill my: ❏ **MC** ❏ **VISA** Credit Card Expiration Date:_____

Card# _____

Cardholder's Signature _____

Name_____

Address_____

City_____State_____Zip_____Country_____

Mail to: Training Resources • 8929 Old LeMay Ferry Rd. • Hillsboro, MO 63050
Please include street address as UPS does not deliver to P.O. boxes.
Please allow 4 - 6 weeks for delivery.
☎ Telephone orders (charge cards only) call: (314) 789-4522, ☎
Monday through Friday, 8:30 - 4:30 CST.